Forensic Science:
IN PURSUIT OF JUSTICE

History of
Science

Essential Library

An Imprint of Abdo Publishing | www.abdopublishing.com

Forensic Science:
IN PURSUIT OF JUSTICE
by L. E. Carmichael

Content Consultant

Dr. Karen S. Scott
Director and Associate Professor of Forensic Science
Arcadia University

History *of*
Science

www.abdopublishing.com

Published by Abdo Publishing, a division of ABDO, PO Box 398166, Minneapolis, Minnesota 55439. Copyright © 2015 by Abdo Consulting Group, Inc. International copyrights reserved in all countries. No part of this book may be reproduced in any form without written permission from the publisher. Essential Library™ is a trademark and logo of Abdo Publishing.

Printed in the United States of America, North Mankato, Minnesota

02014
012015

Cover Photos: Kateryna Larina/Shutterstock Images; Shutterstock Images; Thomas Pajot/Shutterstock Images; Fer Gregory/Shutterstock Images

Interior Photos: Kateryna Larina/Shutterstock Images, 1, 3; Thomas Pajot/Shutterstock Images, 1, 3; Fer Gregory/Shutterstock Images, 1, 3; Shutterstock Images, 1, 3, 7, 15, 20, 27, 34, 62, 67; Jane Gitschier/Wikimedia, 9; Wikimedia, 17, 30, 71; AP Images, 18, 43, 77, 79; Tomatito/Shutterstock Images, 24; Medioimages/Photodisc/Thinkstock, 33; Amelie Benoist/Corbis, 37; US National Library of Medicine, 40; Sean Justice/Corbis, 44; Amy Roh/AP Images, 47; Sarah Davis/AP Images, 51; Pat Vasquez-Cunningham/AP Images, 52; Photick/Isabelle Rozenbaum/Thinkstock, 55; Public Domain, 57; Peter Foerster/AP Images, 61; Johl Threlkeld/AP Images, 65; Kichigin/Shutterstock Images, 73; Jubal Harshaw/Shutterstock Images, 74; Thomas Grimm/AP Images, 81; Tobias Hase/AP Images, 84; Reed Saxon/AP Images, 87; Nick Ut/AP Images, 88; Chris Pizzello/AP Images, 90; Shawn Hempel/Shutterstock Images, 92; Twin Design/Shutterstock Images, 94; Jupiterimages/Thinkstock, 97

Editor: Jenna Gleisner
Series Designer: Craig Hinton

Library of Congress Control Number: 2014943866

Cataloging-in-Publication Data
Carmichael, L.E.
Forensic science: in pursuit of justice / L.E. Carmichael.
p. cm. -- (History of science)
ISBN 978-1-62403-561-6 (lib. bdg.)
Includes bibliographical references and index.
1. Forensic sciences--History--Juvenile literature. 2. Criminal investigation--Juvenile literature.   I. Title.
363.25--dc23

2014943866

Contents

DNA FINGERPRINTING

In November 1983, 15-year-old Lynda Mann left home to visit a friend in Narborough, England. She never arrived. Her body was discovered on a secluded footpath near the village. She had been sexually assaulted and strangled. The crime was shocking and horrific, and people wanted answers. Because locals often used the footpath, police believed the killer lived nearby. Semen found with Mann's body came from a man with blood type A, which is shared by 42 percent of people on Earth.[1] At the time, police had no other evidence and no suspects, so the case went cold.

The Eureka Moment

Six miles (10 km) away, at the University of Leicester, geneticist Alec Jeffreys was working on a method for measuring differences in people's deoxyribonucleic acid (DNA). DNA is a material in all living organisms that contains genetic information.

In 1984, geneticist Alec Jeffreys discovered DNA in each person's blood produces a unique pattern.

FROM MINI TO MICRO: STRs AND CODIS

Jeffreys's DNA fingerprinting method measured minisatellites containing ten to 15 base repeats. Today, most crime labs use microsatellites with core sequences of just two to six bases. Also known as short tandem repeats (STRs), microsatellites are more variable than minisatellites, decreasing the chances two different people will have matching DNA profiles by coincidence. In 1998, the Federal Bureau of Investigation (FBI) launched the Combined DNA Index System (CODIS), a database of DNA profiles collected by different law enforcement agencies. All samples in CODIS have been fingerprinted using the same set of 13 STRs. Except for cases dealing with identical twins, the chance that DNA profiles from different people will match at all 13 STRs is as low as one in 1 trillion people.[2]

Jeffreys, who had once blown up his aunt's apple tree with a toy chemistry set, was especially interested in DNA sequences called minisatellites. Most DNA sequences in human genes are unique arrangements of the bases A, G, C, and T. Minisatellites, in contrast, are composed of a core sequence that is between ten and 15 bases long. The sequence repeats over and over again. The same core sequence appears in many different places in human chromosomes, and Jeffreys believed the number of repeats at a particular chromosomal location might vary from person to person.

To test his theory, Jeffreys purified DNA from blood samples his lab technician and her parents donated. Jeffreys cut their chromosomes into fragments and loaded the pieces into a gel, where electrical current forced them to migrate. Because shorter fragments passed through the gaps in the gel more easily than long ones, the shortest fragments moved the farthest through the gel. This created a picture of the minisatellites, organized by size.

On Monday, September 10, 1984, at 9:05 in the morning, Jeffreys checked his results. "It was an absolute eureka

Check Out Receipt

Canaryville

Tuesday, March 13, 2018 2:44:39 PM

Item: R0444359584
Title: Forensic science : in pursuit of justice
Due: 04/03/2018

Total items: 1

Thank You!

131

Jeffreys pioneered DNA fingerprinting, helping solve more criminal cases with forensic science.

moment,"[3] Jeffreys later said. Each person's DNA had produced a unique pattern of minisatellite bands similar to a supermarket barcode. Even more impressive was that Jeffreys could clearly see his lab technician shared bands with her parents.

This indicated their genetic relationship. "We suddenly realized that we'd essentially stumbled upon a DNA-based method for biological identification,"[4] Jeffreys recalled.

Jeffreys recognized his discovery's potential for forensics. Before it could be used, though, he would have to improve the technique. His first "DNA fingerprints" were a blurry mess and would never hold up to scrutiny in court. It took several months of experimenting to make the process clear and reliable. Another issue was that no one knew how long DNA could survive outside a living person—for example, in stains at a crime scene. "So," Jeffreys said, "I spent the next two days cutting myself and leaving blood marks round the laboratory. Then we tested those bloodstains and found their DNA was intact."[5] His team later discovered they could retrieve DNA from blood and semen samples as much as four years old. They also found a method for separating vaginal cells from sperm cells in semen. This technique would prevent a victim's DNA from contaminating that of her rapist.

DNA Solves a Case

During the following months, Jeffreys used DNA fingerprinting to solve parental disputes and immigration questions. Then, in 1986, he got a phone call about a crime. On July 31, 1986, the body of 15-year-old Dawn Ashworth had been found on a footpath one mile (1.6 km) away from the site of Lynda Mann's murder three years earlier. The new victim had suffered similar injuries. Semen taken from Ashworth's body was also from a man with type A blood, so police believed the same man had committed both crimes. And this time, they had a suspect: Richard Buckland, a teenager with a record of sexual offenses. During interrogation, Buckland confessed to Ashworth's murder but claimed he had nothing to do with Mann's death.

Investigators had read about DNA fingerprinting and asked Jeffreys to prove Buckland had killed both girls. When Jeffreys completed the test, his first thought was that something had gone terribly wrong. DNA from the semen showed the same man had committed both murders, but that man wasn't Buckland. "Then the police did something that I thought was fantastically brave," Jeffreys said. "Rather than disbelieve DNA, they totally believed it and launched what proved to be the world's first DNA-based manhunt, asking for blood samples from men from the entire community."[6]

More than 4,500 men between the ages of 17 and 34 volunteered their blood for the test, but none of them matched the killer's DNA fingerprint. The breakthrough came in September 1987, when a baker named Ian Kelly went for lunch with some friends. At the pub that day, Kelly bragged

DNA IDENTIFIES THE DEAD

Fifty-four women disappeared in Vancouver, Canada, between 1983 and 2001. After a lengthy investigation, police arrested local pig farmer Robert Pickton in 2002. A search of Pickton's property took two years to complete. Using excavators, dump trucks, and a 90-person search team, police uncovered more than 500,000 fragments of hair, bone, teeth, and other potential evidence. The pieces were small because Pickton had dismembered his victims' bodies and fed them to his pigs. The only way to identify the women's remains was through DNA.

Forensic scientists found DNA fingerprints belonging to 33 different women among the evidence. In 2007, Pickton was convicted of six cases of second-degree murder and sentenced to life in prison. Further charges weren't pursued because Pickton had already received the maximum possible penalty under Canadian law.

DNA FINGERPRINT EXCEPTIONS

Most of the time, it doesn't matter whether forensic scientists use a person's blood, semen, or hair as a source of DNA because they all produce the same DNA fingerprint. Chimeras are exceptions to this rule. Chimeras form when the embryos of fraternal (nonidentical) twins fuse before birth, producing one baby. Because that baby began as two separate individuals, different tissues in its body will contain distinct sets of DNA.

If a chimera left hairs at a crime scene, scientists could compare the hair DNA to DNA from the suspect's blood sample, but the fingerprints might not match. A guilty person might go free. Only approximately 100 cases of chimerism have been identified, but no one knows how many chimeras truly exist.

that he had used a fake passport to donate his own blood under the name of Colin Pitchfork. When police caught wind of the switch, they arrested Pitchfork, who confessed to the crimes and the cover-up. Pitchfork's DNA fingerprint was a perfect match for the semen samples from the murders, and on January 23, 1988, he became the first man in history to be convicted of a crime based on DNA evidence. Pitchfork received two life sentences, making him eligible for parole in 2016.

A Forensic Revolution

The Pitchfork case—and Jeffreys's forensic breakthrough—inspired Joseph Wambaugh's best-selling true crime book *The Blooding* and caught the attention of law enforcement groups worldwide. DNA fingerprinting quickly became a tool for analyzing body parts, body fluids, and other types of biological evidence. In 1989, Virginia became the first US state to require collection of DNA samples from convicted sex offenders and other violent criminals. Soon after, police started matching suspects in current crimes to evidence from cold cases. In one example, a prisoner in New York in 2000 was linked to an unsolved murder from 1979. In 2000,

Christopher H. Asplen, executive director of the USA's National Commission on the Future of DNA Evidence, said, "DNA is perhaps our most powerful tool in law enforcement to come along since the fingerprint."[7]

But DNA is not just a tool for identifying the guilty. As the Pitchfork case showed, DNA can also be used to eliminate the innocent. Reflecting on the case that changed his life, Jeffreys said, "I am pretty sure that, given his confession, Buckland would still be in jail today. Worse, the real perpetrator would have gone on to kill again."[8]

The Innocence Project

Defense lawyers Barry Scheck and Peter Neufeld founded the Innocence Project in 1992. Its mission is to use DNA testing to clear people who've been unjustly convicted of crimes they did not commit. As of May 2014, the project had cleared the names of 317 people who had served between five months and 35 years in prison before their innocence was proven. Of those the Innocence Project has freed, 18 had been awaiting execution.

The Polymerase Chain Reaction

DNA breaks down into shorter and shorter fragments when exposed to heat or chemicals outside of the body. Because of this, blood or semen samples found at crime scenes often could not be used for Jeffreys's DNA fingerprinting. The samples simply didn't contain enough good-quality DNA.

The polymerase chain reaction (PCR) solved this problem. Based on the process human cells use to replicate DNA, US biochemist Kary Mullis began developing PCR in 1983. Today, PCR allows forensic scientists to make billions of copies of specific DNA sequences needed for DNA profiling. This increases the number of useable fragments in a decomposed sample, providing a boost that makes analysis much easier.

Using PCR to target short tandem repeats (STRs), scientists can create DNA profiles from samples as small as a single hair root or skin cell. "The DNA has to be in really bad shape for PCR not to work," according to Wayne Murray, one of Canada's foremost forensic geneticists.[9] "So PCR gives us an increased span of cases we can look at and get a result from, and that means, down the road, when we come into court, we're getting a bunch more guilty pleas. Criminals realize they're not going to beat the new DNA."[10]

Mullis won the Nobel Prize for PCR in 1993. Since then, PCR-based methods of DNA profiling have almost completely replaced Jeffreys's original technique.

A technician fills test tubes with DNA samples to perform a polymerase chain reaction.

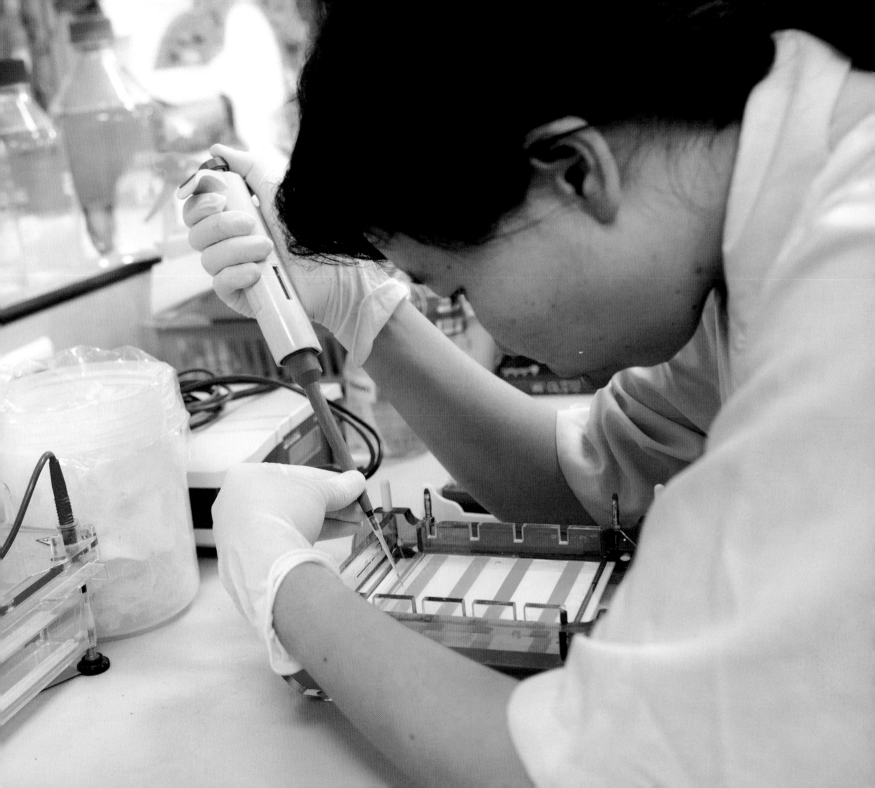

Chapter Two

Bodies of
EVIDENCE

$$\frac{a+b}{a} = \frac{a}{b} = 1.618$$

DNA fingerprinting is a very recent chapter in the history of forensics, which is the use of scientific methods to solve crimes. The word *forensics* comes from the Latin word *forum*, a public gathering. An autopsy was performed on Julius Caesar in 44 BCE. At one forum, Roman physician Antistius announced which of Caesar's 23 stab wounds had actually killed him. The word *autopsy* has its roots in a Greek word meaning "seeing with one's own eyes." Performed today by medical examiners or forensic pathologists, the primary goal of an autopsy is to determine the cause and manner of death, whether it be an accident, a suicide, a homicide, or a natural occurrence. Autopsies establish whether a crime has actually been committed.

The science of autopsy took a long time to develop. For centuries, the Christian church forbade scientists from dissecting human bodies. The first detailed studies of

Early autopsies of the 1500s were often public teaching lessons.

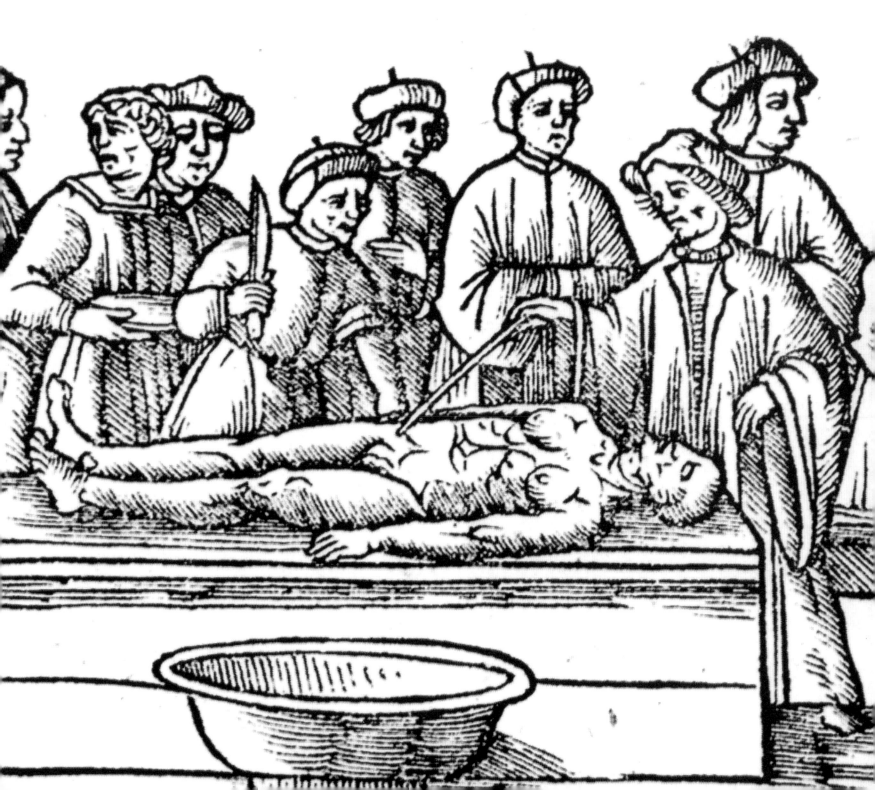

Bernard SPILSBURY

Sir Bernard Spilsbury was born in England in 1877. During his 42 years as a forensic pathologist, he collected evidence at crime scenes, conducted more than 25,000 autopsies, and became the world's first celebrity expert witness. Spilsbury was famous for both his unshakeable integrity and his ability to explain complex scientific evidence using plain language. As one of his contemporaries put it, "[Spilsbury] could achieve single-handed all the legal consequences of homicide—arrest, prosecution, conviction, and final post-mortem—requiring only the brief assistance of the hangman."[1]

Horrified by poor investigative methods that were commonly in use, Spilsbury was also the mastermind behind Scotland Yard's first murder bag. Intended for detectives working crime scenes, a murder bag was a kit including gloves, a magnifying glass, a tape measure, swabs, and everything else needed for properly collecting and preserving forensic evidence.

human anatomy didn't take place until the 1500s, around the time French and Italian governments began asking doctors to help investigate suspicious deaths.

Control over many hospitals transferred from churches to the government in the 1800s. Government-run hospitals permitted doctors to study human remains, helping them expand their knowledge of death. Advances in microscope technology during this time allowed doctors to examine human tissues and cells in greater detail than ever before. Pathologists, such as Great Britain's Sir Bernard Spilsbury, developed new techniques for determining cause of death. These techniques included everything from designing new tools—such as special probes for following wound tracks—to conducting experiments that replicated murders and their effects on human bodies.

The Bone Detectives

A properly conducted autopsy is critical when murder is suspected. In some cases, however, human remains are so badly decomposed that an autopsy is no longer possible. These victims are then examined by forensic anthropologists.

Forensic anthropology developed rapidly in the 1800s. One of the first US investigations hinging on this science took place in 1849. On November 23, Dr. George Parkman disappeared after visiting Professor John W. Webster, a friend who owed him money. A week later, a janitor discovered a decomposing corpse hidden in Webster's Harvard laboratory. Anatomist Oliver Wendell Holmes Sr. concluded the bone fragments investigators recovered matched Parkman's age

and description. Webster was executed for murder, but the verdict was controversial. Many anthropologists at the time believed there wasn't enough information about the human skeleton for Holmes to have made concrete conclusions.

In the following decades, US and European forensic anthropologists launched research projects designed to fill these gaps in their knowledge. Starting from bodies with known identities and characteristics, they found and studied skeletal differences between people of different genders, ages, and ethnic backgrounds. French anthropologist Étienne Rollet was responsible for a major advancement during this period. While measuring the bones of 50 men and 50 women, Rollet discovered consistent relationships between people's heights and the lengths of their femurs, or thigh bones. He then developed a simple formula for estimating total height from skeleton parts, helping forensic anthropologists identify unknown victims.

Additional breakthroughs occurred in the 1900s, due in part to studies of soldiers killed in the Korean and World Wars. The development of the X ray was also key because

From bones and teeth alone, forensic anthropologists can identify a victim and, in many cases, determine cause of death.

TAKING A BITE OUT OF CRIME

US revolutionary Paul Revere may have been the first person to use forensic dentistry. After the Battle of Bunker Hill in 1775, he recognized the remains of his friend Joseph Warren from the silver and ivory dentures Revere himself had made.

"Teeth are terrific," forensic dentist James Berry once said. "Give us one tooth and we just might be able to make an identification. Give us a mouthful, and we can often match suspects to victims, unknowns to names—even evidence items to victims and suspects. They last almost forever. They're well-documented in most cases. They're about the toughest biological evidence available."[2]

A FACE ON EVERY SKULL

Anthropologists use facial reconstruction—a blend of science and art—to determine a victim's appearance based on skull shape. Swiss anatomist Wilhelm His Sr. pioneered the technique in 1895.

In a different application of the technique, US sculptor Frank Bender reconstructed the face of John List, who killed his family and disappeared in 1971. Bender's model showed what List might look like 18 years later. A neighbor of a man called Bob Clark saw the reconstruction on *America's Most Wanted* and called the show, leading to the capture and conviction of List, who had been living under the false name. Today, the Forensic Anthropology Computer Enhanced System (FACES) at Louisiana State University uses a similar aging technique to assist in child abduction cases.

it allowed anthropologists to study bones in greater detail than was possible using microscopes alone.

Today's forensic anthropologists also assist with major crimes such as terrorist attacks. After identifying whether bones are human, anthropologists reassemble skeletons and determine how many victims are present. Further study can reveal a victim's age, sex, and ethnicity, as well as personal medical history, which assists with identification.

The Time of the Crime

During murder investigations, knowing when someone died is just as important as knowing how. Belgian-French physiologist Pierre Nysten made an early attempt at pinpointing time of death in 1811. While studying rigor mortis—the stiffening of bodies after death—Nysten discovered rigor begins in the small muscles of the face approximately three hours postmortem. It spreads to larger muscles until the whole body is affected. Rigor then recedes, following a relatively predictable sequence and schedule.

Twenty-eight years later, English doctor John Davey compared data from the United Kingdom and the tropics to investigate algor mortis, the cooling of human remains. Davey discovered climate, the body part measured, and whether the victim had a fever all affected rates of temperature change after death. Although timetables of rigor and algor mortis provided guidelines for investigators, they did not tell the entire story.

Clearly, more precision was needed. It arrived in 1894 when French entomologist Jean-Pierre Mégnin published *Fauna of the Tombs*. The book describes his studies of flies, beetles, and mites that feed on corpses. The insects colonized, fed, and left when changes in body chemistry significantly altered their habitat. Mégnin observed that "the workers of death only arrive at their table successively, and always in the same order,"[3] allowing him to pinpoint time of death between one day and three years.

One hundred years later, US professor Bernard Greenberg followed in Mégnin's footsteps. An expert on the more than 1,000 members of the blowfly family, Greenberg studied the effect of environmental conditions on the life cycles of corpse-dwelling insects, making time-of-death estimates much more precise. Today, members of the

THE FORENSICS OF TERRORISM

On September 11, 2001, terrorists crashed airplanes into the World Trade Center in New York, killing 2,753 people. It took nine months to recover the victims, during which time their bodies were exposed to sunlight, weathering, fire, and mold. The collapse and its aftermath posed a huge challenge for forensic scientists working to identify bodies.

As of June 21, 2013, there were 21,906 entries in the WTC–Human Remains Database. Most of these remains were too fragmented to be identified using facial features or fingerprints. Even with the combined efforts of pathologists, anthropologists, dentists, and DNA specialists, only 1,638 victims had been identified 13 years later.

American Board of Forensic Entomology use insect life to determine everything from whether a body was moved after death to whether the victim had been poisoned or drugged.

Flies and other insects feed on deceased bodies at certain times, lending scientists clues about a victim's death.

THE BODY FARM

Forensic anthropologist Dr. William Bass founded the Anthropology Research Center at the University of Tennessee Knoxville in 1980. More commonly known as the Body Farm, the center is a 1.3 acre (0.5 ha) wooded lot devoted to researching human decomposition. Since work began, scientists have studied bodies decaying in the open, under water, below ground, in buildings, and in the trunks of cars. So many factors affect decomposition rates that, before the Body Farm, the only way to estimate time of death was with the taking of the body's temperature and an educated guess. Now, timelines are increasingly based on scientific data, improving their accuracy.

Chemical
CLUES

$$\frac{a+b}{a} = \frac{a}{b} = 1{,}618$$

I n the 700s, Arabian physician and chemist Jabir converted metallic arsenic to arsenious oxide, an odorless, tasteless, deadly white powder. Used as a rat poison in the 1800s, the compound was widely available. Except in massive doses, it was undetectable in food or drink, and symptoms of arsenic poisoning closely resembled stomach flu or cholera, a common and often deadly disease at the time. All of this made arsenic hugely popular as a murder weapon. It earned the nickname inheritance powder because so many people used it to kill family members for their money.

Toxicologists founded the field of forensic chemistry. These scientists search for ways to detect arsenic and other poisons in the human body. Work began in the 1700s, but the field got its true start in 1813 when Spanish doctor Mathieu Orfila

Toxicologists have been building on ways to detect poisons in the body since the 1700 and 1800s.

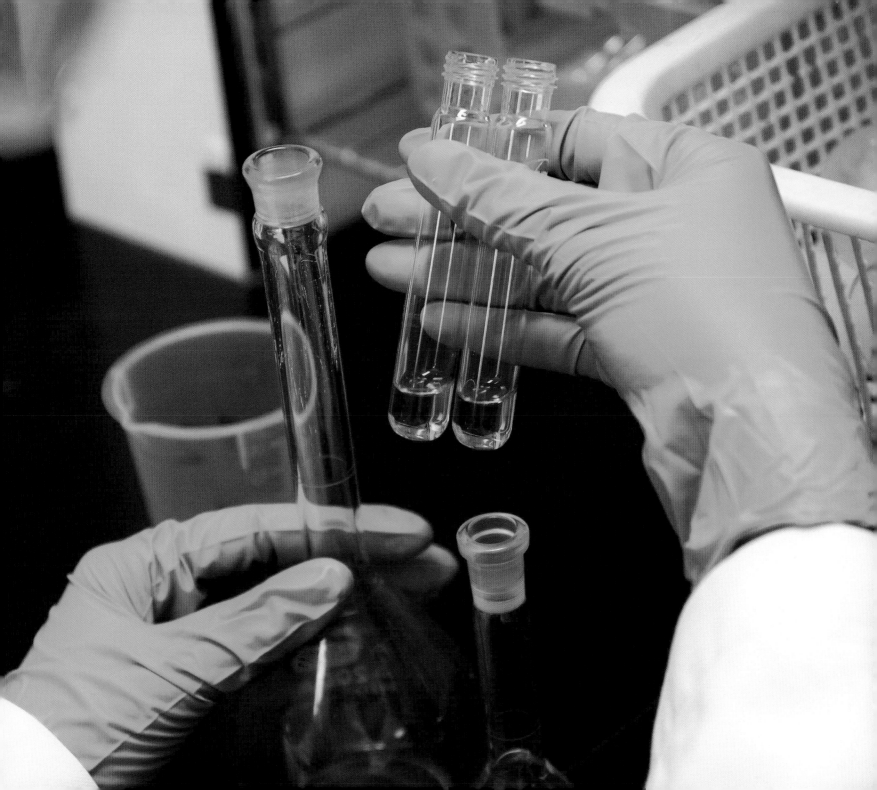

published the groundbreaking book *General Toxicology*. Summarizing all previous knowledge about poisons, the text also describes animal experiments Orfila had done to understand how these chemicals affect living things. Orfila's fame spread throughout Europe, and he is now considered the father of toxicology.

Orfila and others made several attempts to develop a reliable arsenic test. One approach involved converting arsenic into a gas, which then condensed into a stain called an arsenic mirror. Because most of the gas escaped during the process, this test was very insensitive. It was difficult to detect small but still fatal doses, and the method was difficult to explain to juries during murder trials.

The breakthrough came in 1836 when English chemist James Marsh designed a new device for concentrating the arsenic gas. The device was so effective Marsh could detect even the smallest amounts of arsenic in tissue samples from the victim's body. During the 1840 trial of Marie Lafarge, who was accused of poisoning her husband, Orfila demonstrated Marsh's test for the jury. Lafarge was convicted, and with Orfila's stamp of approval, the Marsh test took center stage in arsenic investigations. A modification of the technique is still used today.

From Poisons to Drugs

As tests for arsenic and other metallic poisons developed, murderers of the 1800s switched to plant-based toxins. Plant alkaloids—a group of chemicals including nicotine, caffeine, morphine, and strychnine—were easy to purchase and extremely difficult to detect. Even Orfila believed these alkaloids could not be detected.

His student, Jean-Servaise Stas, disagreed. In 1850, after three months of painstaking analysis, Stas found nicotine in a poisoned victim. It was a major step forward, but Stas's technique had limitations. Human decomposition involves chemical changes, and in some cases, bodies produce cadaveric alkaloids. These chemicals mimicked poisons, such as nicotine, during Stas's test, producing a positive result when the victim had not, in fact, been poisoned. Toxicologists needed tests specific to plant-based alkaloids. They also needed ways to measure how much of a substance was present in human remains. Many potentially deadly compounds were used in lower doses for medical or recreational purposes.

For instance, when the Bayer company (makers of aspirin) launched in 1881, one of the first pharmaceuticals they produced was heroin. At the time, doctors believed heroin would be a good alternative to addictive medicines such as opium and morphine. The health benefits of cocaine were also widely promoted in the 1800s: fictional detective

FEWER DEATHS BY POISONS

Today, only one out of 100 murders in the United States, Canada, and Europe involves poison.[1] This is due in part to the advances in traceability thanks to forensic chemistry. However, accidental poisonings, prescription drug overdoses, and product tampering or contamination cases also require the expertise of toxicologists.

More than 35 million chemicals are recognized by name, and millions more likely exist. But most toxicology labs can only screen for the hundreds to thousands most likely to be involved in criminal investigations. New developments in medical, industrial, and illegal drug chemistry continue to challenge toxicologists.

Sherlock Holmes and real-life psychiatrist Sigmund Freud were both devoted users. At high doses, however, these and newer drugs—such as the methamphetamine prescribed to soldiers during World War II (1939–1945)—were lethal.

Developed in 1896, the Marquis test was one of the first forensic tools specific to plant alkaloids. Toxicologists mix a sample of the suspected drug with formaldehyde and sulfuric acid. Different drugs turn the liquid different colors: methamphetamine turns orange; drugs in the opium family turn purple. Forensic drug testing expanded rapidly after this. By 1955, there were 30 different chemical tests for morphine alone.

New Solutions to Old Problems

Now recognized as harmful, heroin, cocaine, methamphetamine, and many other substances are consequently illegal in many countries. These bans haven't stopped their use, however, and drugs often contribute to other crimes, including traffic accidents, burglaries, assaults,

Stas became the first person to detect nicotine in the body of a poisoning victim.

DRUG TESTS

Two types of tests for illegal drugs exist. Presumptive tests indicate a particular substance might be present. Often conducted by investigators in the field, presumptive tests usually involve color changes. The Marquis test for alkaloid drugs is one example. Presumptive tests never involve smelling or tasting unknown substances, even though these actions are commonly depicted in detective fiction. These methods are not only unsafe and ineffectual, but they also contaminate the evidence.

Presumptive tests are too imprecise to be used as evidence in court, but they provide a starting place for confirmatory tests. Done by specialists in forensic chemistry, confirmatory tests positively identify illegal substances while measuring their concentration, or purity.

THE CHEMISTRY OF ARSON

Accelerants are substances, such as gasoline or kerosene, that make it easier to start a fire. During arson investigations, forensic chemists must determine whether an accelerant was used and what kind. These are difficult questions. Accelerants are complex mixtures to begin with, and during fires, they react with everything that burns. Firefighting chemicals, weathering, and bacterial action further complicate the samples, making analysis both time-consuming and expensive.

In 2014, University of Alberta researchers and Mark Sandercock of the Royal Canadian Mounted Police designed a computer program to analyze GC/MS results in arson investigations. The program can detect chemical signatures of gasoline—the most common accelerant—in just a few seconds. The program "significantly reduce[s] the amount of time it takes for us to process the data for an arson case," Sandercock said. "Like in any other investigation, the sooner [investigators] have the information, the less cold the trail is."[2] Plans to apply the software to other accelerants are already underway.

rapes, and murders. Many cases handled by today's crime labs require drug testing.

Modern forensic chemists face the same challenges with drugs toxicologists of the 1800s faced with poisons: the chemical they are searching for is mixed with many other substances. These mixtures can be relatively simple, such as cocaine that has been cut, or blended, with caffeine. In blood, urine, or decomposing human remains, however, a vast array of compounds is present in a single sample.

A technological breakthrough occurred in 1951. Called gas chromatography, it was the first automatic, mechanical means of precisely separating all the components of a mixture. In the late 1960s, gas chromatography was paired with mass spectrometry. After separation by the gas chromatograph, components of the mixture are bombarded with a stream of electrons in the mass spectrometer. This causes the components to break down in a characteristic way. The instrument then identifies and calculates the amount of every substance present in the sample.

Cocaine and other illegal drugs are often involved in crimes.

In 1971, a team of Swedish chemists proved gas chromatography–mass spectrometry (GC/MS) could identify everything from alcohol to amphetamines in both their pure states and in human tissue samples. The method was sensitive

enough to detect very low levels of illegal drugs and even worked on samples from decayed human remains. There were only two downsides. Chemicals couldn't be identified unless their GC/MS profiles had already been measured and stored in a reference library. And because GC/MS was so sensitive, samples were easily contaminated. Many chemicals diffuse through human skin, so even touching the evidence was enough to change the results. These challenges were easy to overcome, and GC/MS now dominates the field of forensic chemistry. GC/MS is a potent weapon in the war against both murder and drugs.

Environmental Forensics

When the United States began passing environmental protection laws in the 1970s, a new brand of forensic chemistry was born. Environmental forensics involves identifying types of pollutants and tracing them to their sources. GC/MS is a fundamental tool in these investigations, which require isolating and calculating the amount of pollutants in soil and water. While methods for detecting water contamination date back to 1879, GC/MS now makes it possible to detect very small concentrations of pollutants.

Scientists use GC/MS to detect substances in the body.

Firearms
ANALYSIS

$$\frac{a+b}{a} = \frac{a}{b} = 1.618$$

In 1835, policeman Henry Goddard responded to a late-night robbery at a mansion in London. The family's butler, Joseph Randall, said he had been awakened by a masked man who had fired a gun and fled. The bullet was lodged in the headboard of Randall's bed. As Goddard inspected the house, however, he grew suspicious of the butler's story. Pry-marks at the front door were on the inside of the frame, as if someone had tried to break out instead of in. Furthermore, the supposed thief had used a different tool to pry open a cupboard door within the home—an unnecessary complication experienced criminals would avoid. Also, when Goddard examined the bullet from Randall's headboard, he noticed an unusual bump on the bullet.

At the time, gun owners molded their own bullets, and when Goddard inspected the butler's mold, he found a hole that perfectly matched the bump. Confronted with

Firearms analysis has drastically improved due to advances in technology.

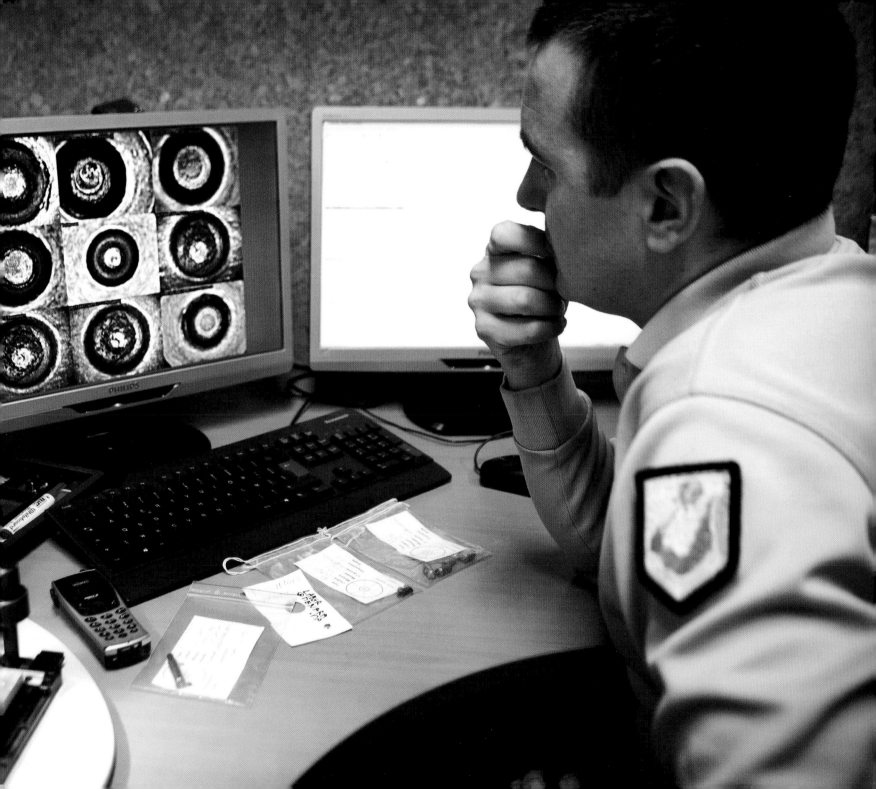

the evidence, Randall confessed. He had staged the robbery, hoping his employers would reward him for protecting their home. It was the first time firearms analysis—the forensic science of matching bullets to weapons—was used to solve a crime.

Staring Down the Barrel

Early firearms were smooth-bore, without any markings inside the barrel. With rare exceptions, such as the Randall case, the only detectable difference between the bullets they fired was caliber, or the diameter of a bullet or gun barrel. Caliber was sometimes enough to solve a mystery. In 1863, for example, investigators proved Civil War General Stonewall Jackson was killed by one of his own men. The fatal bullet was a 67-caliber Confederate ball, rather than the 58-caliber rounds used by Union forces.

Smooth-bore firearms were relatively inaccurate. To improve both precision and power of the shot, late-1700s gun manufacturers switched to oblong bullets instead of balls and added a series of ridges and grooves to the inner surface of gun barrels. Called rifling, this system of ridges and grooves causes the bullet to spin as it exits the gun, much as a football spins in flight.

This innovation became relevant to forensics in 1888 when Parisian doctor Jean Alexandre Eugène Lacassagne removed three bullets from a murder victim during an autopsy. "It was extraordinary," Lacassagne wrote. "The bullet found in the larynx, which had not collided with anything hard, was creased along its axis with the same kind of furrow as the bullet that was lodged in the shoulder. . . . It seemed to be a kind of marking or sign of identity of the revolver."[1] When Lacassagne asked gun expert Charles Jeandet about the marks, Jeandet explained that rifled gun barrels imprinted their ridges and grooves on bullets during firing. Fascinated, Lacassagne fired two test shots from the suspect's gun into the body of a man who had died of natural causes. The markings on the test bullets perfectly matched the ones he had observed on bullets from the victim, suggesting the bullets were fired from the same gun.

The study of rifling marks and their use in forensics advanced in 1912 when Victor Balthazard applied the developing science of photography to firearms analysis. Balthazard photographed bullets, then enlarged the images. This not only made

The Patch and the Paper

Before bullets were packaged in cartridges containing gunpowder, all components necessary for firing had to be added to the gun separately. One such component was the patch, a small piece of cloth or paper. In 1794, English pathologists found a scrap of paper in Edward Culshaw's fatal head wound. The chief suspect was 18-year-old John Toms. When police searched Toms' pockets, they found a sheet of paper with a torn edge that perfectly matched the patch from Culshaw's wound. Toms was convicted of murder.

Jean Alexandre Eugène LACASSAGNE

Dr. Jean Alexandre Eugène Lacassagne (1843–1924) was a forensic science innovator. He was interested in everything from tool marks to time of death to tattoos, which he called speaking scars for what they revealed about people's occupations, politics, and character. Lacassagne launched the Archives of Criminal Anthropology, in which forensic scientists shared their discoveries, and wrote a handbook that helped doctors unfamiliar with investigation conduct better autopsies. During one of his research projects, he identified the ages at which 37 human bones stopped growing and fused together. This helped anthropologists age and identify victims from their skeletal remains.

Lacassagne believed practical research, thorough training, and standardized procedures were critical to forensic investigation, a viewpoint still upheld by the National Academy of Sciences. For his extensive and wide-ranging contributions, Lacassagne is considered a founder of modern forensics.

it easier to identify and document striations on individual bullets, but it was also the first method for comparing two bullets side by side. After this, firearms analysis was increasingly accepted at trials, but it didn't come to prominence until the Prohibition-era gang wars of the United States in the 1920s and early 1930s.

The Saint Valentine's Day Massacre

On February 14, 1929, seven members of George "Bugs" Moran's gang waited in a Chicago, Illinois, warehouse for a truck full of illegal alcohol. Moran himself was running late and arrived just as a police car appeared on the scene. Suspecting rival gangster Al Capone had set him up, Moran fled. His henchmen weren't so lucky. Area residents reported several minutes of sustained gunfire, after which all seven men were discovered dead.

Scandal ensued. The public believed police had murdered the unarmed men. To avoid charges of conspiracy, Chicago authorities asked Calvin Goddard from New York's Bureau of Forensic Ballistics to conduct the investigation.

COMPARISON MICROSCOPES

Counting ridges and grooves can identify a gun manufacturer, but individual markings on a specific gun must be analyzed microscopically. Firearms analysis took a giant leap forward with the invention of the comparison microscope, which allows examiners to view two items at the same time. The first comparison microscopes were built in the 1880s, but 40 years passed before they were seriously applied to forensics. Emile Chamot was most likely the first to use one for bullet examinations in 1922. Calvin Goddard, Charles E. Waite, and Philip Gravelle championed the technology, and by 1931, comparison microscopes had become standard in the field.

At the warehouse, Goddard collected 70 cartridge casings from 45-caliber Thompson machine guns. Using an innovative new comparison microscope, he concluded two guns were involved in the shooting. Goddard test-fired the eight machine guns belonging to the police department and found the rifling marks did not match.

The police were cleared, but ten months passed without a break in the case. When officers raided the home of one of Capone's hit men, however, they discovered two Thompsons. Goddard matched bullets from these guns to those fired at the warehouse, proving the massacre was part of an ongoing gang war.

Goddard's work on the case made such an impression he was appointed director of a new private crime lab in Chicago called the Scientific Crime Detection Laboratory (SCDL). In addition to firearms examination, Goddard offered analysis of blood and fingerprint evidence. When the FBI launched their own integrated crime lab in 1932, their first employee was a man Goddard had trained at SCDL.

Rapid-Fire Comparisons

Firearms comparison was now an established forensic science, but as with DNA and GC/MS analysis, it became truly powerful when linked to a database of known gun and bullet markings. Calvin Goddard's mentor, Charles E. Waite, started the first such database in the early 1900s. Waite's files included caliber, type of ammunition, and the number and twist of the lands and grooves distinctive to every brand of firearm produced in Europe and the United States.

Toxicologist and Assistant Director Dr. Clarence W. Muehlberger works in the crime detection laboratory at the Scientific Crime Detection Laboratory in July 1936.

The next step was building databases for comparing markings specific to individual weapons, a task made much simpler by computers. DRUGFIRE, launched by the FBI in 1989, was the first automated system for firearms comparisons in the United States. DRUGFIRE allowed scientists to check bullets and cartridges found at crime scenes against those linked to previous investigations, making matches to cold cases practical. Since firearms experts only had to check the closest potential matches, the time required for comparisons was significantly reduced. The Bureau of Alcohol, Tobacco, and Firearms established a similar system called IBIS. In 2000, IBIS and DRUGFIRE were merged to form the National Integrated Ballistic Information Network (NIBIN). NIBIN is still used for firearms analysis today. In addition to matching bullets to weapons, today's firearms experts can estimate firing distance, restore damaged serial numbers, and detect gunpowder residue on suspects' hands.

Measuring the size of bullet holes helps firearms analysts determine the range at which the shots were fired.

DETECTING DISTANCE

One way to estimate the distance from which shots were fired is to measure the size of the bullet holes and the pattern of gunpowder burns. In 1903, English scientist E. J. Churchill did one of the first experiments using this method. Four years earlier, someone had shot Mrs. Camille Holland in the head with a 32-caliber revolver. Using a similar gun and ammunition, Churchill fired test shots into sheep skulls from various distances. By comparing the damage on the sheep skulls to that on Holland's, Churchill proved the fatal shot was fired from six to 12 inches (15 to 30 cm) away.

Written in
BLOOD

$$\frac{a+b}{a} = \frac{a}{b} = 1.618$$

O n average, the adult human body contains ten pints (4.7 L) of blood, some or all of which may be spilled during a violent crime. When a suspicious stain is discovered at a crime scene, forensic scientists must answer three questions: Is the stain blood, is it human blood, and whose blood is it?

Historically, it was difficult to answer the first question just by looking because blood changes color and texture over time. As a result, there was a lot of interest in developing chemical tests to distinguish blood from stains such as rust and paint. The breakthrough came in 1863 when Christian Schöenbein showed hydrogen peroxide reacts rapidly with hemoglobin, the part of blood that gives it its red color. This reaction produces bubbles of oxygen. For the first time, investigators could prove stains on a suspect's clothing really were blood.

Those studying forensic science often create mock crime scenes to practice analyzing blood spatter and possible sequences of events.

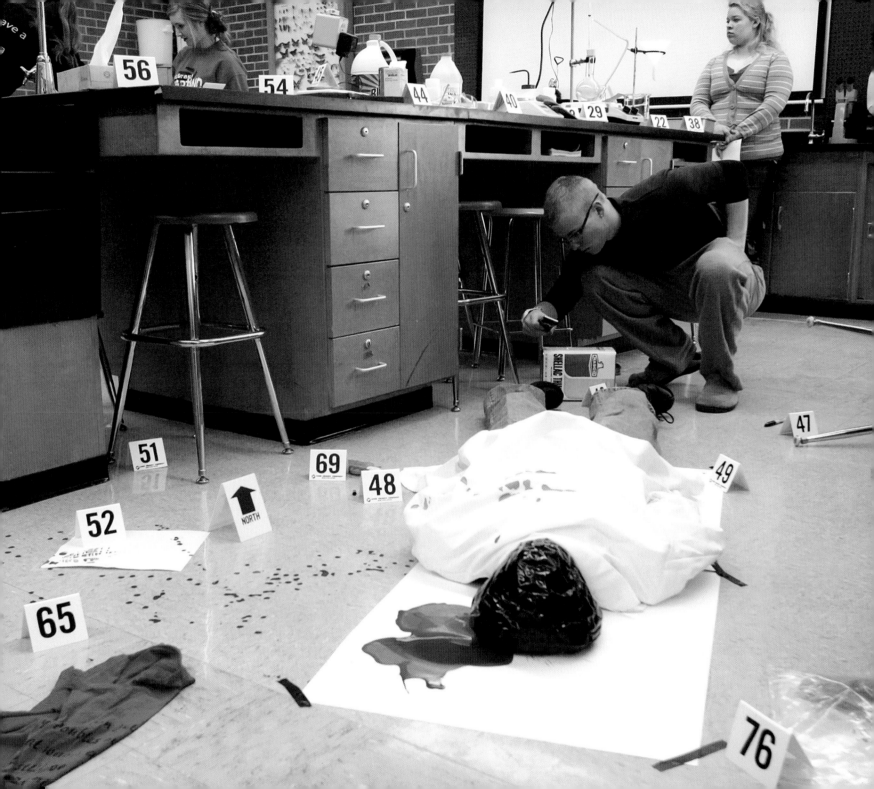

Criminals adapted quickly, however, claiming the blood came from animals they had butchered for food. At a time when many people raised their own livestock, this excuse was hard to disprove. In 1901, German scientist Paul Uhlenhuth found the solution. When Uhlenhuth injected rabbits with a small amount of human blood, the rabbits' immune systems produced antibodies that attacked the foreign cells. If he then added blood from immunized rabbits to a sample of human blood, the antibodies caused the human sample to clump. Uhlenhuth repeated the process, using blood from common food animals to create antiserums that reacted with cow, pig, sheep, and goose blood, among others.

"It is noteworthy," Uhlenhuth wrote when announcing his discovery, "that, after drying blood samples from men, horses and cattle on a board for four weeks and dissolving them in [salt] solution, I was able to identify the human blood at once using my serum—a fact that should be of particular importance for forensic medicine."[1] He was right: his test worked on the small, old stains often found at crime scenes, making it incredibly useful to investigators. Uhlenhuth himself was one of the first to apply the discovery, leading to the conviction of a serial child killer.

Around the same time as Uhlenhuth's breakthrough, Austrian scientist Karl Landsteiner took the first step toward matching bloodstains to their human donors. He discovered distinctive proteins that marked the surfaces of blood cells, defining four blood types: A, B, O, and AB. Since an individual person has only one kind of blood cell, simple tests to detect these proteins allowed police to eliminate suspects whose blood didn't match the type found at a crime scene.

Max Richter was the first to apply ABO blood testing to a criminal case in 1902. Unfortunately, he was unsuccessful. Landsteiner's method only worked on samples containing intact blood cells, meaning it couldn't be used on old stains in which the cells had broken down. Fourteen years later, Italian scientist Leon Lattes developed a test that worked on stains, making blood typing practical for forensic use. Tests for ABO and other proteins were the standard method of blood analysis until Alec Jeffreys discovered DNA fingerprinting in 1984.

IT'S BLOOD . . . OR IS IT?

The Kastle-Meyer test for blood was developed in the early 1900s. An improvement on Schöenbein's hemoglobin method, the test produces a pigment called phenolphthalein in the presence of hemoglobin. In 1908, scientists got a positive reaction from a 26-year-old bloodstain. Because of its power and convenience, the Kastle-Meyer test is still used today.

It's a presumptive test only, however, because phenolphthalein is also produced by substances other than blood. Saliva, pus, vegetable extracts, and even some metallic compounds all produce false positives, so further testing must be done to confirm a stain is blood.

The Blood Whisperers

Even before chemical tests for blood were developed, forensic scientists realized the shapes, patterns, and locations of blood smears could help reconstruct the events surrounding a crime. In the 1840s, British toxicologist Alfred Swain Taylor published some of the first discussions of blood spatter evidence. Taylor's topics included bloody footprints, arterial spray, changes to color and clotting, and how stains could reveal whether bodies were moved after bleeding injuries occurred. In one case he investigated, Taylor proved a woman was attacked at the top of a staircase rather than having accidentally fallen to her death.

Taylor's work was based on experience rather than formal scientific study. Austrian doctor Eduard Piotrowski conducted the first systematic experiments on blood spatter in 1895. Victor Balthazard made the next major breakthrough in 1939 when he discovered the length and width of blood drops varied according to impact angle, or the angle at which they had struck a surface. This allowed scientists to identify a point of origin, an important clue when reconstructing attacks.

In this 2003 case, blood spatter expert Duane Deaver argues a woman was beaten to death after studying the blood spatter and patterns at the crime scene.

A sensational US investigation brought blood spatter analysis into the spotlight.

On July 4, 1954, Marilyn Sheppard was found beaten to death in her own bed.

Scientists measure blood marks to determine their angle of origin.

Her husband, Dr. Sam Sheppard, claimed his injuries came from fighting with Marilyn's attacker, who had escaped. When police discovered Mr. Sheppard had been having an affair, however, he became their chief suspect.

The attack had been savage. Marilyn's bedding and walls were coated in blood. At the trial, coroner Samuel Gerber testified that one bloody pillowcase contained the impression of a surgical instrument. Although Gerber had never identified a matching instrument, casting doubt on his interpretation of the evidence, Sam Sheppard was convicted. Years later, however, the Supreme Court concluded extensive media coverage had biased both investigators and jury members. They ordered Sheppard be released and given a new trial.

This time, the outcome was different. Shortly after his initial conviction, Sam's lawyers had hired Paul Kirk to reexamine the evidence. Kirk was a highly respected pioneer in the field of blood spatter analysis. Based on the blood evidence, Kirk reconstructed Marilyn's attack. Unlike Sam, Marilyn's killer was left-handed and had used a blunt weapon, not a surgical knife. Even more telling, Kirk found a stain in the Sheppard house that didn't match Sam or Marilyn's blood type. After hearing Kirk's testimony during the 1966 retrial, the second jury found Sam not guilty of his wife's murder. The case captured the public's attention and even inspired the television show and film *The Fugitive*, but Marilyn's true killer was never found.

SEARCHING FOR OTHER BODILY FLUIDS

Blood is not the only body fluid commonly found at crime scenes. In sexual assaults, for example, semen is important evidence. Semen contains an enzyme called acid phosphatase. In the 1950s, forensic scientists developed a chemical test for this enzyme that produces a color change when semen is present. Because low levels of acid phosphatase are also found in saliva, feces, and male urine, the enzyme test is presumptive only. To confirm the presence of semen, forensic scientists look for sperm cells under a microscope. The Christmas tree stain makes sperm much easier to identify. This dye turns the heads of sperm red, their middle portion blue, and their tails yellow-green. It also turns skin cells blue-green. This helps analysts distinguish sperm cells from vaginal cells during rape investigations.

Chapter Six

No More
MISTAKEN IDENTITY

$$\frac{a+b}{a} = \frac{a}{b} = 1,618$$

D uring the Industrial Revolution of the 1800s, Europeans moved away from farms and into cities. As cities grew, crime rates increased, and with so many strangers around, it became harder for victims and witnesses to positively identify criminals. Making matters worse, lawbreakers often changed their names and appearances to avoid detection. It became so difficult to identify repeat offenders that French police officers received a bonus if they managed it. This would change in the late 1800s due to documentation of human features and fingerprint identity.

Alphonse Bertillon worked for the Paris police. A thin man prone to migraines and nosebleeds, he was frustrated by the ineffective methods his department used to track repeat offenders. Bertillon believed every person had physical characteristics impossible to modify or hide. Precise measurements of these traits, including the

Fingerprints, which are unique to each person, are often key pieces of evidence at crime scenes.

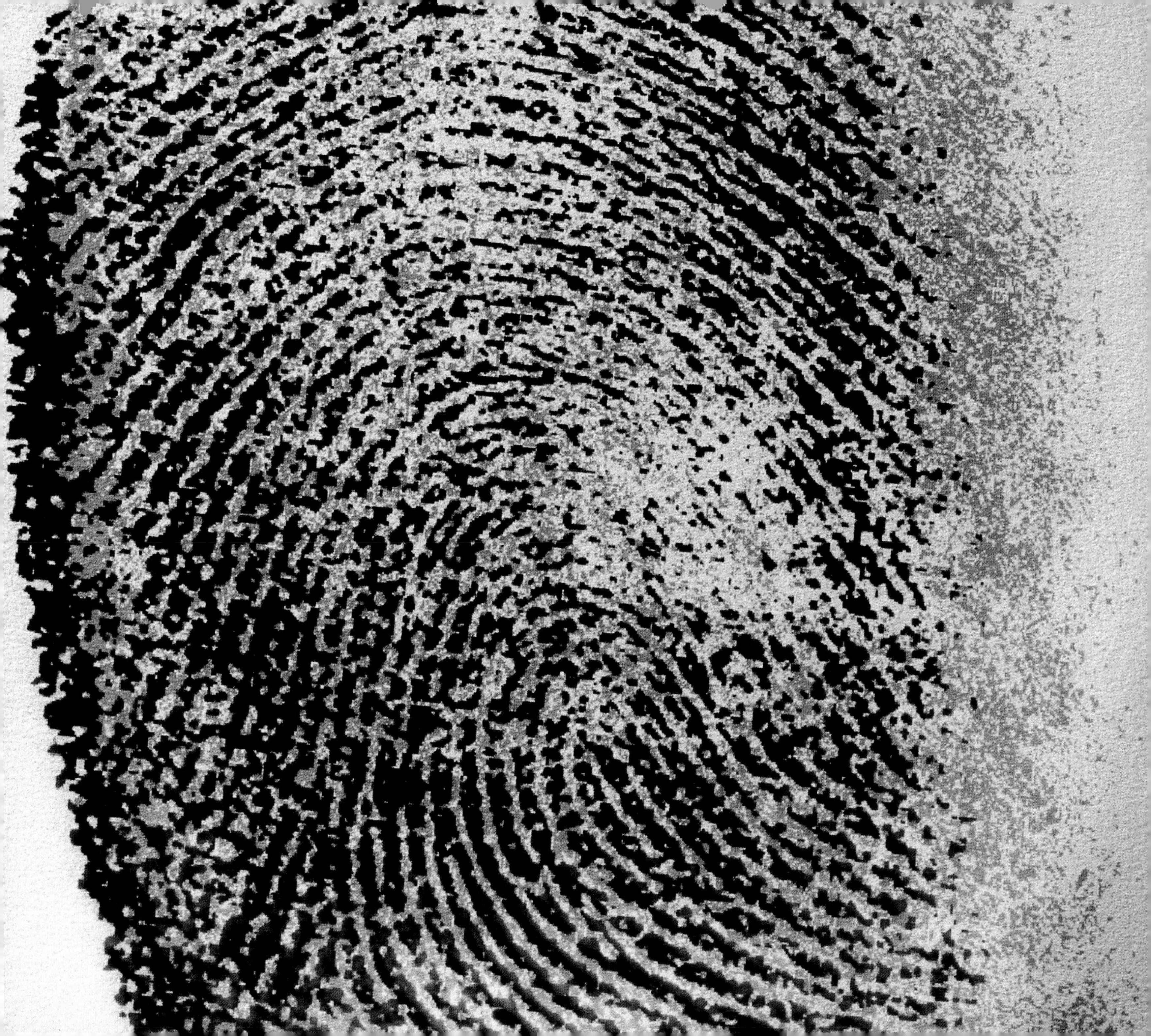

length of a finger or width of the jaw, could make definitive identifications possible no matter what kind of moustache a criminal grew.

Using instruments accurate to within one millimeter (0.04 inch), Bertillon took a series of 11 to 14 measurements from convicted criminals—enough data, he believed, that no two people would share identical profiles. He also designed a new, streamlined filing system, which sped up comparisons of a suspect's measurements to those of known offenders.

At first, no one took him seriously, but Bertillon was relentless. Eventually, the police agreed to a test. Bertillon would have three months to prove his method could identify a repeat offender. During the trial period, his team measured more than 1,500 suspects. A week before the deadline, Bertillon found a match. A man calling himself Dupont matched every measurement for Martin, a repeat offender. The trial was a success.

Called anthropometry, meaning "the measurement of man," Bertillon's method identified 300 repeat offenders in the first year. In 1883, Paris police adopted the method and it quickly spread around the world.

From Fingers to Fingerprints

The first use of fingerprints in criminal investigations most likely dates to China's Tang Dynasty, 618 to 906 CE. One thousand years passed before Western scientists

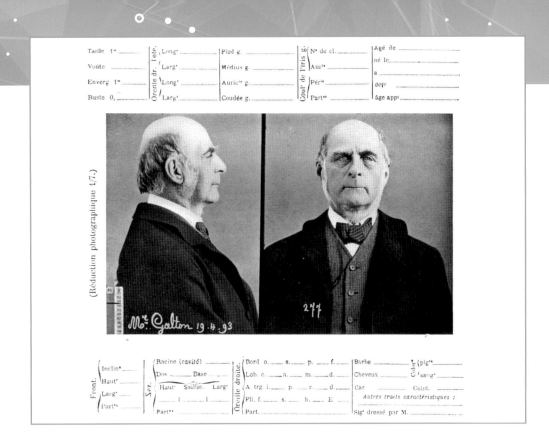

Bertillon's descriptive method of anthropometry helped identify hundreds of repeat offenders.

recognized the patterns on fingertips—and the traces they left on surfaces—could be used to identify criminals. Even then, law enforcement groups were reluctant to listen. In 1877, for example, when British officer William Herschel suggested identifying criminals in India by their fingerprints, Inspector General Sir James Bourdillon dismissed his idea as a crazy man's obsession.

PERMANENT MARKERS

After sorting fingerprints into arches, whorls, and loops, forensic scientists examine the places where skin ridges branch and come together. French scientist Edmond Locard discovered the unique arrangement of sweat pores along these ridge lines could also be useful in identification, especially when evidence prints were incomplete.

While studying these pores, Locard tried altering his own fingerprints by burning his hands with irons or hot oil. Locard—and notorious career criminals such as bank robber John Dillinger— quickly discovered these painful techniques have no lasting effect. Ridges and pores arise from deeper, underlying layers of skin, so they regrow as the surface layer heals.

Attitudes toward fingerprints began changing in 1880 when Scottish doctor Henry Faulds correctly identified a burglar by dusting latent fingerprints. Francis Galton, an English scientist and cousin of Charles Darwin, learned of this work and was fascinated. He contacted Herschel, who in 1888 generously forwarded all of his fingerprint records for Galton to study. These records were the basis of Galton's 1892 book *Fingerprints*, the first definitive work on patterns in human fingerprints.

But the utility of fingerprints was limited without a practical method of classifying and organizing the records. Building on Galton's work, head of the Metropolitan Police of London Edward Henry developed a classification method based on three basic shapes: whorls, loops, and arches. In 1901, Henry established the Fingerprint Branch of Scotland Yard's Criminal Investigation Division. That year, forensic scientists using anthropometry caught 500 repeat offenders. In 1902, more than 1,500 were caught using fingerprints.

Fingerprints had several advantages over anthropometry as a method of identification. Anthropometry required precise measurements made by highly trained workers using expensive equipment. In contrast, fingerprinting required nothing but ink and paper, and prints could be successfully collected by almost anyone. In addition, as Bertillon himself admitted, anthropometry couldn't be used on growing children, whose body shape constantly changed, or women, whose hairdos complicated height measurements.

A bigger issue, though, was that anthropometry could only be used if police had a suspect in custody. To be truly powerful, a forensic method of identification needs to work on evidence found at crime scenes, such as fingerprints. This was demonstrated during a famous case in 1911. By this time, Bertillon had begun adding fingerprint information to his records, but the files were still organized according to body measurements. A repeat offender named Vincenzo Peruggia stole the *Mona Lisa* from France's Louvre museum, leaving only fingerprints as evidence. Bertillon didn't find the man in his files until two years later, after a witness tip had already led to an arrest. In an identification system based on fingerprints alone, a match could have been made in about half an hour. This, along with many other advantages, quickly made fingerprinting the standard method of identifying criminals worldwide.

Finding Clues in Fingerprints

In 1892, Juan Vucetich of Argentina used fingerprints to prove Francisca Rojas had killed her two children in order to marry her younger lover. Due to Vucetich's success, Argentina made fingerprinting the cornerstone of its criminal investigation system in 1896, five years before Scotland Yard did the same.

The Perfect Match

Three-year-old June Devaney was a patient at Queen's Park Hospital in England when she disappeared on May 15, 1948. Her body was found on hospital grounds two hours later. Under June's bed, police discovered a water bottle that had been taken from a nearby supply cart. Fingerprints on the bottle didn't match any of the Queen's Park staff. Police solved the murder by collecting fingerprints from every local man over the age of 16. Belonging to 22-year-old Peter Griffiths, the 46,253th set was a perfect match. Griffiths confessed and was hanged that November.

Next Generation Identification

Fingerprints identify unknown suspects more often than DNA evidence. This is partly due to two advances: new powders and processes for collecting fingerprints from a wide range of surfaces and computerized databases.

In 1973, the Royal Canadian Mounted Police became the first law enforcement group to computerize its fingerprint records. The FBI's Automated Fingerprint Identification System (AFIS) followed two years later. Computers not only allow fingerprints to be digitally stored and searched, but they also dramatically reduce the time required to find a match. From 1984 to 1985, for example, a serial killer known as the Night Stalker terrorized Southern California. The Los Angeles Police Department (LAPD) had just uploaded its 1.7 million fingerprint records to AFIS, and when it discovered a print in a suspect's car, the computer found a match in just a few minutes. Using visual comparisons, a human fingerprint expert would have needed approximately 67 years to do the same thing.

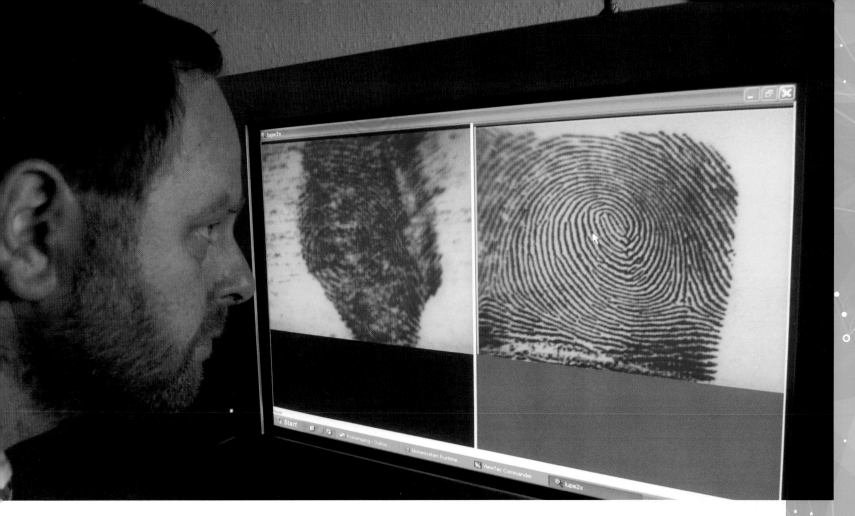

Computerized databases contain millions of different fingerprints and are easily and quickly accessible.

The improved Integrated Automated Fingerprint Identification System (IAFIS) launched in 1999. It contains fingerprint records for more than 75.9 million criminals, as well as their criminal records, mug shots, scars and tattoos, physical descriptions,

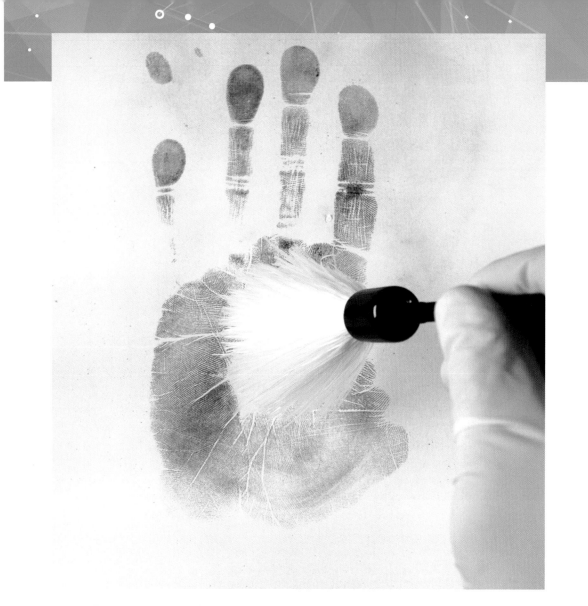

Today, fingerprints identify unknown suspects at least ten times as often as DNA evidence.

and known aliases. US and international law enforcement agencies submitted 23,029 prints to IAFIS in November 2013 alone. That same month, the system identified 25,955 criminals.

In 2014, the database Next Generation Identification (NGI) replaced IAFIS. The FBI's updated system has reduced wait times, returning results on high-priority searches in just ten minutes. In addition to fingerprint checks, it allows automated searches of mug shots, voiceprints, and iris scans, radically advancing the forensics of identification.

THE ARM IN THE SHARK

On April 25, 1935, a tiger shark in a Sydney, Australia, aquarium suddenly began thrashing in what looked like agony. A few moments later, it threw up a human arm. The arm was well-muscled and tattooed with two sparring boxers, but these details weren't enough to make an identification. Due to damage from the shark's digestive system, the hand was very fragile. Despite this, forensic scientists managed to remove small patches of skin, which they reassembled to study the fingerprints. The arm belonged to James Smith, who had disappeared on April 8 after telling his wife he was going fishing with Patrick Brady. Brady, a known drug trafficker, claimed a second man named Reginald Holmes had committed the murder. Holmes, meanwhile, blamed Brady. While Brady was in police custody, Holmes was also murdered. Smith's killer was never found.

Fingerprints on Firearms

When people load guns, they often leave fingerprints on the cartridges surrounding the bullets. However, heat and friction generated during firing usually destroy this evidence. In 2008, John Bond of the University of Leicester developed a revolutionary technique for fingerprinting brass cartridge casings after firing. The method takes advantage of the fact that salts and oils in fingerprints corrode the metal. The technique involves three steps. First, the cartridge must be heated to 1,291 degrees Fahrenheit (700°C), which enhances the corrosion reaction. Then 2.5 kV of electricity is passed through the shell while powder is applied. The powder bonds to the corroded area. Lastly, the cartridge is heated again, this time to 302 degrees Fahrenheit (150°C), baking on the powder and increasing the durability of the print.

Unlike DNA and other types of evidence that degrade over time, corroded fingerprints never go away. "For the first time," Bond said, "we can get prints from people who handled a cartridge before it was fired. Wiping it down, washing it in hot soapy water makes no difference."[1] In 2009, *BBC Focus* magazine voted Bond's technique an invention most likely to change the world. Between 2008 and 2010, the technique had already been applied to approximately 100 cold cases worldwide.

A bullet is examined under a microscope, revealing possible fingerprints and other identifying markings.

$$\frac{a+b}{a} = \frac{a}{b} = 1,618$$

Never
WITHOUT A TRACE

In May 1958, 16-year-old Gaetane Bouchard told her father she was going shopping in Edmundston, New Brunswick, Canada. When she didn't come home, Mr. Bouchard contacted Gaetane's older boyfriend, John Vollman, who lived across the border in Maine. Vollman said he hadn't seen Gaetane since they had broken up. Shortly after, Bouchard found his daughter's body in a local gravel pit where couples often parked. Witnesses recalled seeing Gaetane in a green car with Maine license plates. At the scene, police found tire tracks and flecks of green paint, which presumably chipped off when the vehicle sped away. A search of Vollman's car revealed paint damage that matched the size and shape of the fragments found at the scene. In the glove compartment was a half-eaten chocolate bar bearing smudges of Gaetane's lipstick.

Trace evidence, such as clothing fibers left on a seat or lipstick marks left on a glass, link suspects and victims to crimes.

PAINT AND PDQ

During hit-and-run investigations, chips and smears of vehicle paint are critical pieces of evidence. In the 1970s, scientists with the Royal Canadian Mounted Police showed vehicle models could be identified from their paint chemistry. Today, the RCMP's Paint Database Query (PDQ) system is the largest of its kind in the world. Containing information on 74,000 layers of paint and 20,000 layer combinations applied by car manufacturers, PDQ is used by trace analysts in 26 countries.[1]

First, scientists perform infrared microspectrometry, identifying the chemical makeup of paint layers in an unknown sample. They submit the results to PDQ and the computer searches for the closest matches. An expert then confirms the match, identifying manufacturer, model, and year of production. The database also estimates the probability of the match based on how many vehicles with a particular paint combination were produced.

The key evidence in the case, however, was a hair found grasped in the girl's hand. Forensic scientists studied it using neutron activation analysis. This technique fires atomic particles at evidence samples, making them radioactive. The type of radiation produced showed what kinds and amounts of chemicals were present in the hair. Results showed a sulfur to phosphorus ratio of 2.02 in hairs from Gaetane's head, but the ratio of the hair in her hand was 1.02. This proved the mystery hairs belonged to someone else, most likely Gaetane's attacker. When Vollman's hairs were analyzed, their sulfur to phosphorus ratio was 1.07. This ratio was similar enough to the mystery hairs to identify Vollman as the killer. He was the first person convicted of a crime based on neutron activation evidence.

Every Contact Leaves a Trace

The paint, lipstick, and hairs found in the Bouchard investigation are examples of trace evidence—tiny items with big power to link suspects, victims, and crime scenes. Edmond Locard championed trace evidence in the early 1900s.

A student of Jean Lacassagne's in France, Locard was a huge fan of Sherlock Holmes novels. In these stories, the most insignificant-seeming details were key to cracking the case. Locard believed perpetrators of every type of crime take something with them or leave something behind. Today this idea is called Locard's Principle, but at the time, police dismissed Locard's theories.

With a microscope and some reference books, Locard launched his own crime lab in 1910. His chance to prove the value of trace evidence soon followed. Police had identified suspects in a counterfeiting investigation but found no proof of their guilt. Locard requested the men's clothing. He used tweezers to remove larger particles, then brushed the garments across white paper, collecting dust particles. After examining the dust under a microscope, Locard used chemical tests to identify tin, antimony, and lead in the sample. These metals matched the blend in the fake coins, and the suspects confessed.

INVENTING THE CRIME LAB

Locard's lab was the first dedicated purely to forensic science. It was also the first to offer a range of services under a single roof. In 1914, Dr. Wilfrid Derôme, who had spent two years studying forensics at the University of Paris, established the first such lab in North America in Quebec, Canada. The LAPD followed suit in 1924, and Chicago's Scientific Crime Detection Laboratory opened a few years later. The FBI, established July 26, 1908, didn't have its own crime lab until 1932.

Other remarkable successes followed, validating trace analysis as a forensic science. "Yet, upon reflection," Locard wrote in 1930, "one is astonished that it has been necessary to wait until this late day for so simple an idea to be applied as the collection, in the dust of garments, of the evidence of the objects rubbed against, and the contacts which a suspected person may have undergone. For the microscopic debris that covers our clothes and bodies are the mute witnesses, sure and faithful, of all our movements and all our encounters."[2]

Big Tools for Tiny Evidence

Trace analysis never would have been possible without the invention of the microscope in the 1600s. By Locard's time, microscope technology had improved dramatically, increasing both magnification and clarity of the image.

In the 1930s, inventors began experimenting with a new type of microscope—one that didn't use light. In a scanning electron microscope (SEM), electrons bounce off a sample's surface, creating high-resolution, 3-D images of even the tiniest clues. The prototype SEM was destroyed in an air raid during World War II. After the war, British electrical engineer Sir Charles Oatley revived the technology, which became available in the 1960s.

By this time, scientists were already combining microscopy with light-based spectrometry. This form of spectrometry was invented in 1859 when two German scientists discovered visible light scatters when passing through a substance.

Scanning electron microscopes are capable of picking up images of the smallest trace particles on crime scene evidence.

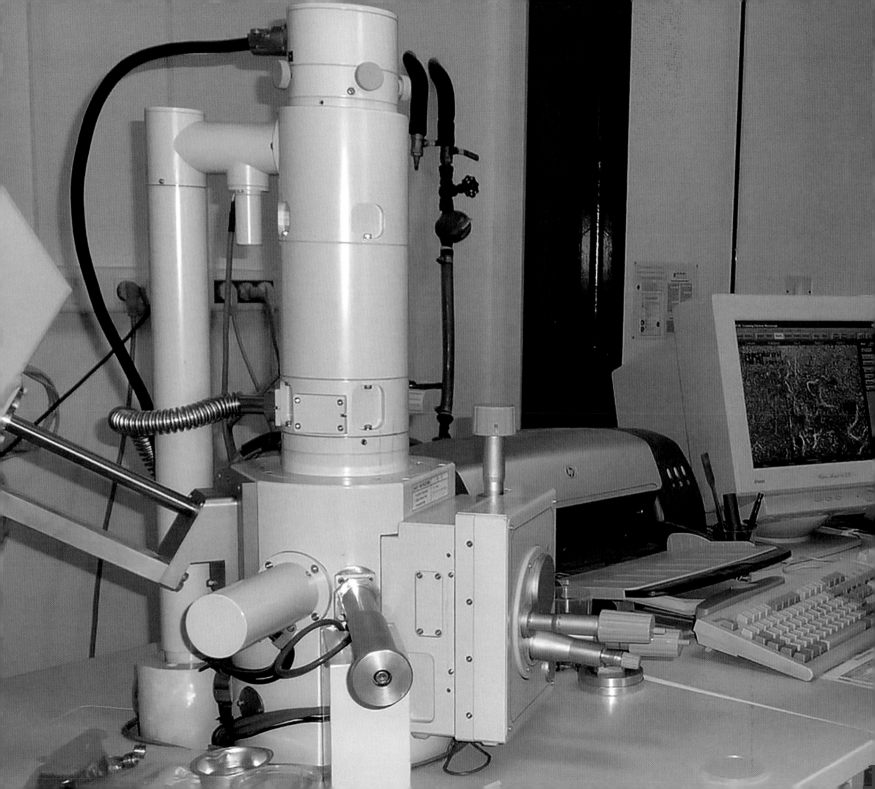

Different substances produce distinct wavelengths, allowing analysts to match unknowns with reference samples. In the 1940s and 1950s, it became possible to use ultraviolet and infrared light for microspectrometry, expanding the types of samples that could be analyzed. Infrared light, for example, is used to identify synthetic fibers such as nylon and rayon.

Before a sample can be processed, it has to be found. In the late 1980s, John Watkins of the National Research Council in Canada developed a new portable laser for crime scene investigation. Called the Luma-Lite, Watkins' device causes fingerprints, bloodstains, and fibers to fluoresce, making them easier to find and collect. In one case involving a fatal hit-and-run car accident, the Luma-Lite revealed a 0.08 inch (2 mm) thread stuck in the car's front grill even after the car had been washed and waxed.

Hairy Details

Trace specialists analyze tiny samples of glass, dust, pollen, paint, and seeds, but fibers and hairs are most common. Fibers found on a victim or at a crime scene could originate from the suspect's carpets, clothing, or car upholstery. And as Locard noted, transfer goes both ways—fibers from the victim's home or clothing are often found on the suspect.

Guidelines for distinguishing between fibers and hairs existed as early as 1866, but it wasn't until 1910 when French forensic scientists Victor Balthazard and Marcelle

Hairs and fibers, such as those from carpet or clothing, are the most common samples of trace evidence.

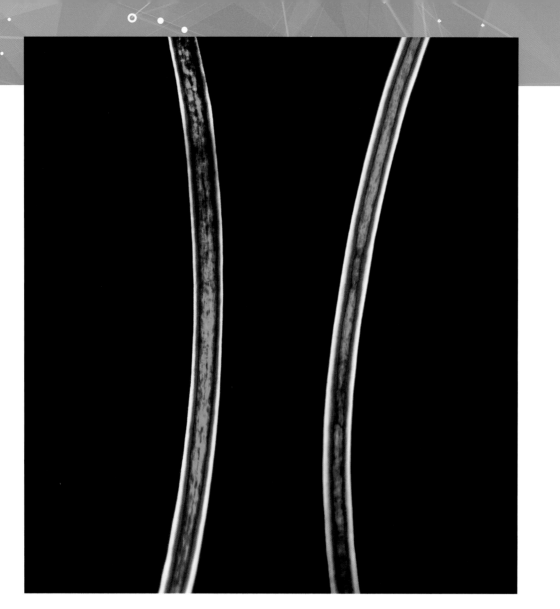

Differences in human and animal hairs help distinguish who or what was at a crime scene.

Lambert published the first comprehensive study on the differences between human and animal hairs. This was important because hairs from wild or domestic animals can link people to crime scenes.

Trace evidence is considered class evidence, which means it can be matched to groups but usually not individuals. For example, fibers found on a murder victim can match a suspect's carpeting without proving the victim was in the suspect's home. After all, many people purchase the same type of carpet. Because of this limitation, trace evidence is best used to exclude possibilities rather than confirm them.

WILDLIFE FORENSICS PROTECTS ENDANGERED SPECIES

The same forensic techniques applied to crimes against people can also be used to investigate crimes against wildlife. Bonnie Yates, a hair specialist with the US Fish & Wildlife Service Forensic Laboratory, developed a new method for identifying an endangered species.

Shahtoosh is a type of wool woven from the underfur of the Tibetan antelope. After China occupied Tibet, road construction gave hunters easy access to antelope, which are now endangered. Sale of shahtoosh is prohibited worldwide, but a single shawl is worth thousands of dollars on the black market. When caught, smugglers usually claim their shawls were legally made from cashmere goats.

Yates discovered that under the microscope, antelope hairs look as if they're packed with pebbles, while goat hairs have dark, solid cores. Yates' work has made it possible to convict shahtoosh smugglers worldwide.

From Page
TO SCREEN

$$\frac{a+b}{a} = \frac{a}{b} = 1.618$$

S pecialists in questioned documents analyze fake passports, threatening letters, phony checks, forged signatures, and many other types of written evidence. The field of document analysis developed largely in the United States. Albert S. Osborn, author of the 1910 manual *Questioned Documents*, pioneered this branch of forensics and applied it in one of history's most famous kidnappings. Charles Lindbergh Jr. was the infant son of celebrity aviator Charles Lindbergh, who had made the first solo flight across the Atlantic Ocean in 1927. On March 1, 1932, the baby vanished from his nursery. Fourteen ransom notes arrived, all containing unusual phrasings and spellings, suggesting English was the writer's second language. The Lindberghs paid $50,000 in gold certificates to the kidnapper, but on May 12, a trucker found the baby's skeletal remains. Charles Jr. had died of a massive skull fracture, an injury pathologists believed occurred the night of the kidnapping.

In 1932, the kidnapping of Charles Lindbergh Jr. and the ransom notes that followed sparked investigation into document analysis.

SEEN THIS BABY?

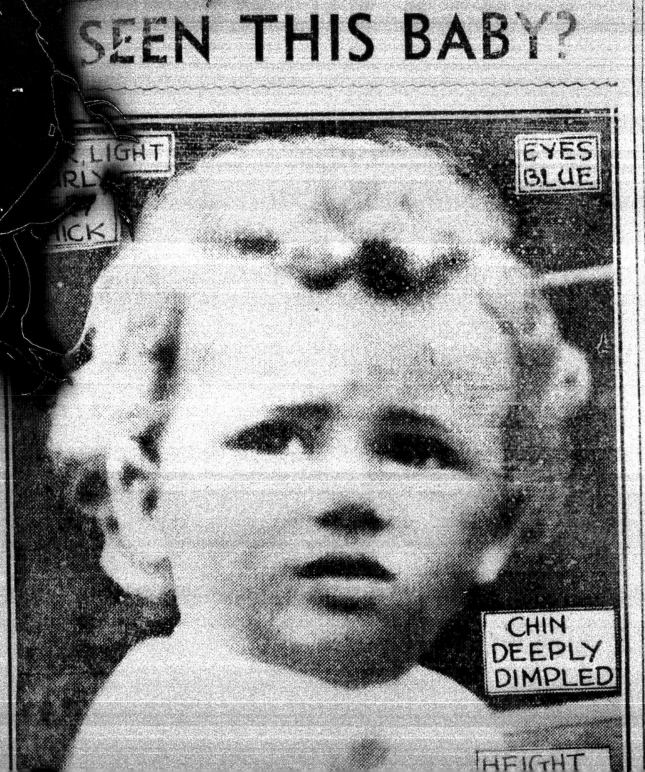

LIGHT
RLY
ICK

EYES
BLUE

CHIN
DEEPLY
DIMPLED

HEIGHT

RA
GIV
DAY

N&C a
Up S
Lind

For
tory, th
major
Broạdc
Colum
are rem
to ann
the sea
fant.

SPEC

Both
have a
appara
frequel
newspa
cials
networ
in the

New York
is with
ils. 'If you
a baby since
notify the

e marks of

pronounced
hin.

an aversion
at he whim-
away if they
him.

Phone

invariably at-
ion. When
ll attempt to

The investigation floundered until September 15, 1934, when a gas station manager reported a German man who had paid in gold certificates. When police raided Bruno Hauptmann's house, they found more ransom money, but Hauptmann said his friend Isidor Fisch was behind the kidnapping. Fisch couldn't deny this accusation because he had recently died.

Osborn and his son Albert D. Osborn examined the ransom notes, finding unique variations in the shape and spacing of letters, proving one person had written them all. To determine whether Hauptmann was the author, they needed a known sample of his handwriting, called an exemplar. Exemplars must have similar content to questioned documents so the spellings and word formations can be properly compared. Osborn Sr. gave police a sample paragraph to use, but the police violated standard procedure when collecting the exemplars. In addition to forcing Hauptmann to write for hours on end, they made him copy different styles of writing. Making matters worse, "I was told to write it exactly as it was dictated to me," Hauptmann said," and this included writing words spelled as I was told to spell them."[1]

As a result, the Osborns found more variation among the handwriting in Hauptmann's exemplars than between some of the samples and the ransom notes. They first concluded a definitive match wasn't possible, but after the ransom money was discovered in Hauptmann's home, Hauptmann was convicted and executed.

Professional writing expert Samuel Small compares ransom notes from the Lindbergh kidnapping case.

The boy is on Boad Nelly
it is a small Boad 28 feet
long two person are on the
Boad the are innosent.
you will find the boad between
Horseneck Beach and gay Head
near Elizabeth Island.
N—"this writer has a habit of making the small 'n's' out of slant with back-hand stroke."
P—"is made with a downward stroke merely the loop no higher than rest of word."
R—"too long in proportion, the same in ransom notes and Hauptmann writing."

In the 1980s, a German company spent $2.3 million US dollars for the right to publish newly discovered diaries attributed to Adolf Hitler.[2] Found by Nazi document collector Konrad Kujau, the diaries revealed Hitler had never wanted the Jews to be eliminated, just relocated.

When the diaries' authenticity was questioned, three experts concluded the handwriting they contained matched exemplars from Hitler. Under UV light, however, investigators discovered a paper additive manufacturers only began using after 1954. The ink also contained chemicals developed after the diaries were supposedly written. Police soon discovered Kujau had a long history as a forger and had also written the Hitler exemplars used for comparison. He served three years in prison for fraud.

Evidence in the Lindbergh case is still debated, but most forensic experts agree Hauptmann was guilty. Either way, this high-profile investigation helped establish questioned document analysis as a specialty of forensic science.

The Evidence of Ink

While handwriting cannot always identify individuals, ink analysis can help identify forgeries. Forgers often alter the content of an existing document, but some inks contain iron, which remains on the page even after it has been erased and overwritten. This iron fluoresces under ultraviolet light, becoming visible to the naked eye. Albert D. Osborn was one of the first to apply this technique in the early 1930s.

Contemporary examiners use infrared light to detect multiple inks in the same document, another sign of possible forgery. Ink ingredients can also be separated with GC/MS, then matched to reference libraries of known blends from different brands and models of pens. The Forensic Services Division of the US Secret Service Laboratory in Washington, DC, has one of the biggest databases of ink references in the world.

Using questioned document analysis, specialists discovered the Hitler diaries were a forgery.

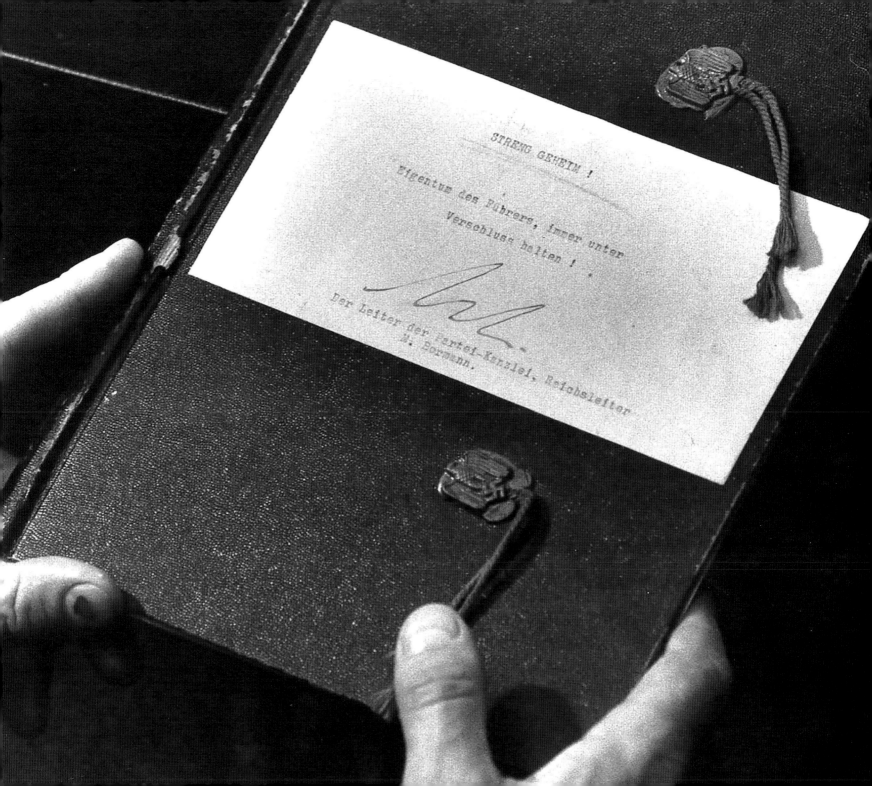

During GC/MS analysis, a small sample of ink is cut out of the document for analysis. This alters the evidence, which is a major disadvantage, especially in cases involving historically significant documents. In 2006, Roger Jones and his team tested a new method of ink analysis called Direct Analysis in Real Time (DART). Using low levels of radiation, DART evaporates tiny samples of ink off the surface of the page before sending them to a mass spectrometer for identification. Because DART sampling takes place outside of the mass spectrometer, there is no need to fold or cut the document. This method is both quicker and less destructive than GC/MS and distinguishes all but the most similar types of inks.

Cybercrime and Digital Forensics

It's hard to imagine a time when computers and their digital descendants weren't embedded in every aspect of human life. When first developed in the 1960s, however, computers filled entire rooms and required special training to operate.

After they became practical for personal use in the late 1970s and early 1980s, a new type of crime emerged.

Initially, law enforcement agencies didn't take computer crimes seriously. Scientists who pursued computer crimes used their personal time and money to develop evidence collection techniques. The earliest tools were based on industry methods for recovering files users had accidentally deleted. As new cybercrimes became possible—such as credit card fraud, blackmail, money laundering, identity theft, child pornography, and pirating of copyrighted content—forensics specialists had to invent new techniques for capturing, preserving, and analyzing digital evidence. Because formal training and support weren't available, groups of investigators banded together to share their knowledge. One group in Baltimore, Maryland, dubbed themselves the Geeks with Guns.

In 1984, the FBI handled only three cases involving digital evidence. Between 1996 and 2008, arrests for cybercrime increased by 950 percent.[4] As law enforcement veterans Michael Knetzger and Jeremy Muraski wrote in their 2008 book *Investigating High-Tech Crime*, "What once

DEFENDING THE DATA

Digital evidence is easily altered or destroyed, compromising investigations. To avoid this, forensic scientists go to extreme lengths to preserve data. Chemicals used to develop fingerprints or test for blood can damage electronic devices, so digital evidence is always recovered first. To protect cell phones against remote wipes (signals which erase data from a distance), cell phones are normally stored in special metallic bags that block incoming and outgoing transmissions. In a pinch, cleaned-out metal paint cans can also be used to block signals.

required criminals to work in disguise, under the cover of darkness, or forcefully take from another can now be done from the comfort of their homes with little threat to their own personal safety. Why engage in a risky bank robbery where the average take is less than $5,000 when you can pull off a high-tech identity theft from your living room and make an average of $10,200?"[5]

This explosion of criminal activity thrust digital evidence to the forefront of forensic investigation. "Digital forensics was once a niche science that was leveraged primarily in support of criminal investigations," cybersecurity specialist Nicole Beebe said in 2009, "and digital forensic services were utilized only during the late stages of investigations after much of the digital evidence was already spoiled. Now digital forensic services are sought right at the beginning of all types of investigations. . . . Even popular crime shows and novels regularly incorporate digital evidence in their story lines."[6]

Cybercrime includes identity theft, credit card fraud, and pirating of copyrighted content.

BY THE NUMBERS

In 1975, Canadian accountant Bob Lindquist launched a new company devoted to what he called forensic accounting. His team uses traditional accounting techniques to search for evidence of fraud and other financial crimes. "Eighty percent of the work in forensic accounting is the same drudgery as in any other accounting, just digging for numbers," Lindquist said. "But the other 20 percent . . . gives us a chance to do something other accountants never experience. It gives us a chance to play detective."[7]

The Future
OF FORENSICS

$$\frac{a+b}{a} = \frac{a}{b} = 1,618$$

On June 12, 1994, Ronald Goldman and Nicole Brown Simpson were found stabbed to death outside Simpson's Los Angeles home. Nicole's ex-husband, O. J. Simpson, had a history of domestic violence and quickly became the primary suspect. When police found blood smears at Simpson's house and on his car, they arrested him for murder.

Simpson, an actor and football star, hired a powerhouse legal team including well-respected forensic scientists. The LAPD had collected 857 pieces of evidence. But at trial, Simpson's team proved sloppy forensics had compromised much of the evidence. Among a host of other problems, one bloodstain collected at the scene contained EDTA, a chemical labs use to prevent clotting. This fact suggested police may have planted a critical piece of evidence.

A prosecutor points to evidence presented during the O. J. Simpson trial.

O. J. Simpson was found not guilty of criminal charges after evidence involved with his case was tampered with.

Broadcast on live television, the Simpson trial exposed the LAPD to public humiliation and sent shockwaves through the forensics community. Simpson was found not guilty, and his case emphasized a truth: forensic science is only credible and effective when evidence collection, handling, analysis, and interpretation are done correctly and honestly.

Forensics on Trial

Though it received ample media attention, the Simpson case was not the first and only example of misconstrued or manipulated forensic evidence. Legal standards for defining an expert witness have since been established in the field of forensic science, but the precision and reliability of the science itself has also been questioned. One reason for this questioning is the fact that different labs use different techniques to answer the same forensic questions. Most troubling are the incompetent or even corrupt forensic scientists whose poor procedures, false reports, and biased testimony continue to impact hundreds of cases. According to the Innocence Project, untested or improper forensic science was involved in 49 percent of the convictions their work has since overturned.[1]

STANDARDS OF EVIDENCE

In 1917, psychologist William Marston invented the polygraph, or lie detector, which is a device for measuring changes in blood pressure. Accused murderer James Frye passed the test but was convicted when the courts ruled this evidence inadmissible in 1923. In a decision that came to be known as the Frye Test, the judges stated the polygraph had not yet gained general scientific acceptance. Many US courts have now replaced the Frye Test with the Daubert Standard. Under Daubert, individual judges can choose to allow evidence gathered using new forensic techniques as long as the method is based on solid scientific practice and principles.

The 1948 founding of the American Academy of Forensic Sciences was an attempt to address these issues. The academy's goals included improving the quality of expert testimony, thus increasing legal and public confidence in the power of forensics. In some ways, the academy succeeded too well. Public fascination with forensics has grown to the point where many jurors believe it to be much more powerful than it really is.

To narrow the gap between perception and reality, the National Academy of Science recommended in 2009 that all types of forensic science be reviewed and overhauled. The proposal included evaluation of new and existing techniques, increased training for practitioners, and a universal handbook of standard procedures.

Digital Forensics

Despite scientific and legal challenges, forensic science continues to change and improve. Forensics must evolve because as fast as advances are made, criminals find ways around them. These evasive maneuvers range from wearing

Known as the CSI effect, jurors often expect cases to reflect those seen in television shows, such as *CSI: Crime Scene Investigation*.

THE CSI EFFECT

"Jurors now expect us to have a DNA test for just about every case," Oregon lawyer Josh Marquis said in 2005. "They expect us to have the most advanced technology possible, and they expect it to look like it does on television."[2] One consequence of this CSI effect is instead of explaining forensic techniques, expert witnesses must teach juries how real-life forensics differs from that in stories. Another result is mounting backlogs at crime labs. Because jurors expect forensic evidence at trial, investigators who once collected five items at a crime scene are now submitting 50 to 400. Not everyone is convinced the CSI effect actually exists, however. A 2008 study, for example, showed little relationship between jurors' desire for forensic evidence and the chance they would convict.

gloves to avoid leaving fingerprints to adding encryptions, preventing investigators from reading data files.

Digital forensics is facing the biggest challenges of any specialty. A single forensic specialist can no longer be familiar with all of the devices, operating systems, and apps he or she will encounter on any given day. Cloud storage and the sheer size of modern hard drives have also dramatically increased the volume of data to be examined. In 2007 alone, the FBI's Computer Analysis and Response Team (CART) processed more than 2.5 petabytes, or 2.5 million gigabytes, of digital evidence.[3]

As cybercrime specialist Simson Garfinkel believes, "[Digital forensic] research needs to become dramatically more efficient, better coordinated, and better funded if investigators are to retain significant [forensic] capabilities in the coming decade."[4] On the wish list are programs capable of automating the retrieval and analysis of data, reducing the need for manual review of content.

Digital forensics may be nearing a crisis point, but breakthroughs in other specialties continue. One example is Arpad Vass's invention: the Light-weight Analyzer for Buried Remains and Decomposition Odor Recognition. Usually called LABRADOR, the

Chain of Custody

In 1891, Austrian lawyer Hans Gross advocated for what is now referred to as chain of custody. The person who collects the evidence marks a label with date and time, location found, description, and unique ID number. The record is updated any time the evidence is transferred, examined, or altered for analysis. An unbroken chain of custody is essential during trials because it suggests no one could have tampered with the evidence.

Chain of custody, a method of documenting everything about a piece of evidence, helps ensure evidence is not tampered with.

device checks for 30 kinds of airborne chemicals produced by corpses. When paired with trained cadaver dogs, LABRADOR simplifies location of human remains. In 2010, police used it to find the body of a woman who had been missing for nine years.

In 2013, Dr. Meez Islam's team at Teesside University in the United Kingdom designed a camera that measures wavelengths of light reflecting off bloodstains. It can detect blood smears invisible to the naked eye and distinguish between blood and other substances. Because aging blood changes color in predictable ways, the camera can also date the stains. In initial testing, estimates for fresh stains were accurate to within an hour; month-old samples were accurate to within a day. Islam's device could be used to establish time of death right at the scene of the crime. Compared to traditional methods that require several days, this is a significant advancement. His team believes the technology can also be expanded for use on other body fluids, such as saliva, sweat, and semen.

Information retrievable from DNA samples is also expanding. Manfred Kayser's team at the Erasmus University Medical Center in Rotterdam in the Netherlands has developed a typing system called HIrisPlex, which predicts a person's hair and eye color from DNA left at crime scenes. Unlike fingerprinting, which is useful only if police have a suspect in custody or a match in a database, HIrisPlex can narrow the list of potential perpetrators. Most important for forensics, "The test is very sensitive," Kayser said, "and produces complete results on even smaller DNA amounts than usually used for forensic DNA profiling."[5]

Evidence of cybercrimes is now found on everything from cell phones and MP3 players to video game consoles and e-readers.

ANY SCIENCE CAN BE FORENSIC

In the right circumstances, almost any science can be used to answer legal questions:

+ Forensic psychologists assess the mental health of victims and witnesses involved in crimes. They are often required to judge whether a criminal is fit to stand trial or if he or she knew his or her actions were wrong at the moment of the crime.

+ When buildings, bridges, and other structures fail, forensic engineers find the causes of the collapse, be they wind, snow, faulty construction, or explosions.

+ Forensic geologists may authenticate gemstones in fraud cases or identify the origin of soil collected during investigations. A forensic geologist who had done fieldwork in Afghanistan located the rocky outcrop appearing in terrorist leader Osama bin Laden's video communications following the September 11, 2001 terrorist attacks.

Forensic evidence is just one of many types of evidence applied to criminal investigations, but many believe it is also extremely powerful. "This is evidence that does not forget," Paul Kirk wrote in 1953. "It is not confused by the excitement of the moment. It is not absent because human witnesses are. *It is factual evidence.* Physical evidence cannot be wrong; it cannot perjure itself; it cannot be wholly absent. Only in its interpretation can there be error."[6] Forensic scientists are doing everything in their power to ensure these interpretations are made with integrity and to the highest professional and scientific standards.

Integrity and truthful handling of evidence will ensure forensics will continue gaining ground in investigations and trials.

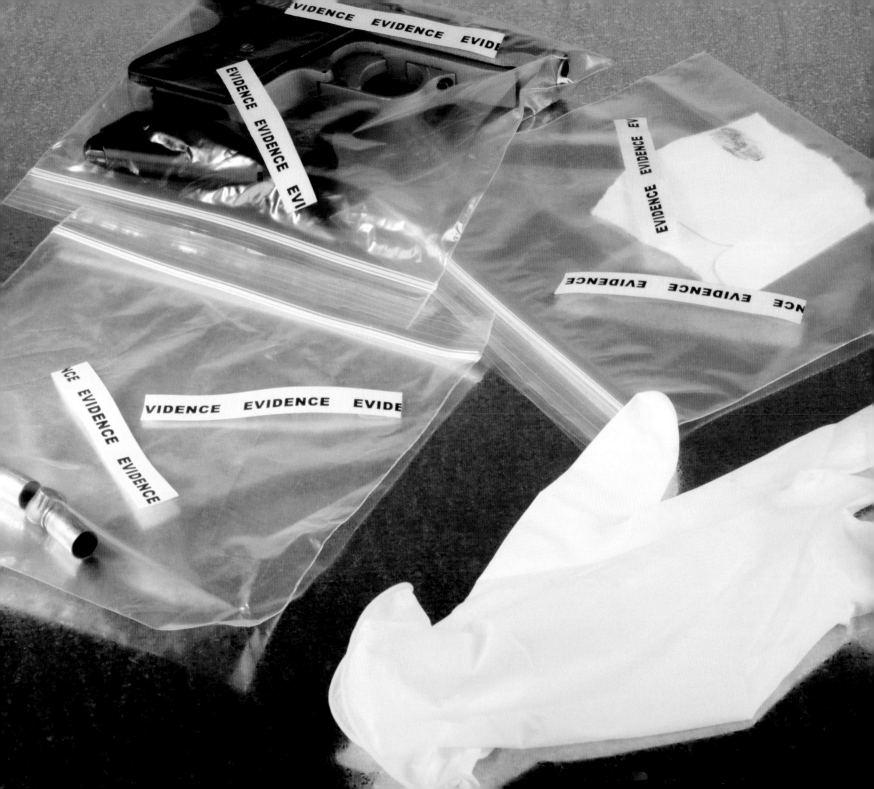

Timeline

44 BCE Antistius conducts the first recorded autopsy on murder victim Julius Caesar.

1247 CE Sung Tz'u's book *The Washing Away of Wrongs* describes one of the first uses of blood evidence in a murder investigation.

1775 Paul Revere identifies a body using dental evidence.

1835 Henry Goddard becomes the first person to solve a crime using firearms evidence.

1836 James Marsh develops a simple and powerful test for detecting arsenic in the human body.

$$\frac{a+b}{a} = \frac{a}{b} = 1{,}618$$

1863 Christian Schöenbein invents the first chemical test for blood.

1883 Alphonse Bertillon proves anthropometry works by identifying a repeat offender.

1896 The Marquis Test for illegal drugs is developed.

1901 Edward Henry launches the Fingerprint Branch of Scotland Yard's Criminal Investigation Division.

1910 Edmond Locard founds the first scientific lab dedicated purely to forensics.

1931 Following the Saint Valentine's Day Massacre of 1929, the comparison microscope becomes standard for comparing rifling marks.

1934 Handwriting analysis is instrumental in solving the Lindbergh kidnapping case.

1958 Neutron activation analysis for trace evidence is accepted in court for the first time.

1966 Paul Kirk's analysis of blood spatter evidence suggests Dr. Sam Sheppard did not kill his wife.

1988 On January 23, Colin Pitchfork is the first person convicted using DNA fingerprinting.

1992 Barry Scheck and Peter Neufeld form the Innocence Project, using DNA evidence to clear the falsely convicted.

2006 DART is tested as a nondestructive method of analyzing ink in questioned documents.

2009 The US National Academy of Sciences recommends overhauling every field of forensic science.

2014 Next Generation Identification replaces iAFIS, making non-DNA-based forensic identification more powerful than ever before.

ential Facts

KEY TECHNOLOGIES

DNA Fingerprinting

Discovered by Alec Jeffreys in 1984, DNA fingerprinting has revolutionized methods for identifying individuals. Using DNA fingerprinting, scientists are able to identify suspects or criminals by blood, semen, saliva, sweat, or hair samples.

DRUGFIRE, IAFIS, and CODIS

Computer databases such as DRUGFIRE, IAFIS, and CODIS have significantly reduced the time it takes to search for matching evidence and have helped close cold cases.

Gas Chromatography-Mass Spectrometry (GC/MS)

Developed in the 1950s and 1960s, GC/MS identifies chemicals in the human body. GC/MS has revolutionized forensic chemistry, trace, and questioned document analysis.

IMPACT ON SCIENCE

Forensic science has helped prosecute criminals, clear innocent suspects, and solve crimes. It has helped develop fingerprinting, firearms analysis, and drug testing—technologies that can be used outside the world of crime investigation. Advancements such as DNA fingerprinting have changed what we know about our own genetic makeup and the ways in which many forms of DNA can identify a single human being.

KEY FOUNDERS OF FORENSICS

Jean Alexandre Eugène Lacassagne

Lacassagne is considered a founder of modern forensics. His 1888 discovery of rifling marks sparked the modern science of firearms analysis. During his research, he created the *Archives of Criminal Anthropology,* in which forensic scientists shared their discoveries. He also wrote a handbook for conducting better autopsies and identified ages at which bones stop growing, helping anthropologists age and identify victims from skeletal remains.

Sir Bernard Spilsbury

Sir Bernard Spilsbury collected evidence at crime scenes and conducted tens of thousands of autopsies in the late 1800s and early 1900s. Spilsbury was also the creative force behind Scotland Yard's murder bag. A murder bag included many of the tools still used to collect forensic evidence, such as gloves, a magnifying glass, a tape measure, and swabs.

QUOTE

"Digital forensics was once a niche science that was leveraged primarily in support of criminal investigations . . . and digital forensic services were utilized only during the late stages of investigations after much of the digital evidence was already spoiled. Now digital forensic services are sought right at the beginning of all types of investigations. . . . Even popular crime shows and novels regularly incorporate digital evidence in their story lines."

— *Nicole Beebe, cybersecurity specialist, 2009*

Glossary

antiserum

A liquid containing antibodies which recognize and attack foreign cells; used to identify human blood.

arterial spray

High-pressure blood spatter caused when arteries are severed during a violent attack.

chromosome

A package of DNA that comes in a matching pair (people inherit one copy of each pair from each parent).

cold case

A crime that remains unsolved due to a lack of evidence during the original investigation.

degrade

Chemical breakdown of evidence due to age or hostile environmental conditions.

entomologist

A scientist who studies insect life.

enzyme

A protein that assists with chemical reactions inside living creatures.

forensic anthropologist

A scientist who applies the study of human skeletons to forensic and legal questions.

forgery

The crime of falsely copying or creating a document to deceive people.

hemoglobin

Iron-containing protein in red blood cells that transports oxygen throughout the body.

larynx

The voice box.

latent fingerprint

A print which is invisible unless powders or chemical processes are applied to develop it.

postmortem

Time since death; also another term for autopsy.

striation

A tiny parallel groove found in firearms and tool mark identifications.

$$\frac{a+b}{a} = \frac{a}{b} = 1{,}618$$

Additional Resources

Selected Bibliography

Owen, David. *Hidden Evidence: 50 True Crimes and How Forensic Science Helped Solve Them*. 2nd ed. Buffalo, NY: Firefly, 2009. Print.

Ramsland, Katherine. *Beating the Devil's Game: A History of Forensic Science and Criminal Investigation*. New York: Berkley, 2007. Print.

Starr, Douglas. *The Killer of Little Shepherds: A True Crime Story and the Birth of Forensic Science*. New York: Knopf, 2010. Print.

Further Readings

Carmichael, L. E. *Fuzzy Forensics: DNA Fingerprinting Gets Wild*. Edmonton: Ashby-BP, 2014. Print.

Lynn, Peppas. *Forensics: The Scene of the Crime*. New York: Crabtree, 2015. Print.

Websites

To learn more about History of Science, visit **booklinks.abdopublishing.com**. These links are routinely monitored and updated to provide the most current information available.

The International Association of Computer Investigative Specialists
PO Box 2411
Leesburg, VA 20177
888-884-2247

http://www.iacis.com
Volunteers of the International Association of Computer Investigative Specialists train and certify workers in forensics computer science.

National Forensic Science Technology Center
8285 Bryan Dairy Road, Suite 125
Largo, Florida 33777
727-395-2511

http://www.nfstc.org
The National Forensic Science Technology Center works to provide forensic training, research, assessment, and technology assistance to those involved in the fields of forensics.

Source Notes

Chapter 1. DNA Fingerprinting

1. Max M. Houck and Jay A. Siegel. *Fundamentals of Forensic Science.* 2nd ed. Burlington, MA: Academic, 2011. Print. 261.

2. Ibid. 271.

3. Robin McKie. "Eureka Moment That Led to the Discovery of DNA Fingerprinting." *The Guardian.* Guardian News and Media Limited, 2009. Web. 12 May 2014.

4. Nick Zagorski. "Profile of Alec J. Jeffreys." *Proceedings of the National Academy of Sciences of the United States of America* 103.24 (2006): 8919. Print.

5. Robin McKie. "Eureka Moment That Led to the Discovery of DNA Fingerprinting." *The Guardian.* Guardian News and Media Limited, 2009. Web. 11 Nov. 2013.

6. Nick Zagorski. "Profile of Alec J. Jeffreys." *Proceedings of the National Academy of Sciences of the United States of America* 103.24 (2006): 8919. Print.

7. "National Law Enforcement Summit on DNA Technology Proceedings." *NCJRS.* National Criminal Justice Reference Service, July 2000. Web. 12 May 2014.

8. Robin McKie. "Eureka Moment That Led to the Discovery of DNA Fingerprinting." *The Guardian.* Guardian News and Media Limited, 2009. Web. 11 Nov. 2013.

9. Jack Batten. *Mind Over Murder: DNA and Other Forensic Adventures.* Toronto: McClelland & Stewart, 1995. Print. 247.

10. Ibid.

Chapter 2. Bodies of Evidence

1. Douglas Starr. *The Killer of Little Shepherds: A True Crime Story and the Birth of Forensic Science.* New York: Knopf, 2010. Print. 85.

2. Colin Evans. *The Father of Forensics: The Groundbreaking Cases of Sir Bernard Spilsbury, and the Beginnings of Modern CSI.* New York: Berkley, 2006. Print. 121–122.

3. Alan Axelrod and Guy Antinozzi. *The Complete Idiot's Guide to Forensics.* 2nd ed. New York: Penguin, 2007. Print. 163.

Chapter 3. Chemical Clues

1. David Owen. *Hidden Evidence: 50 True Crimes and How Forensic Science Helped Solve Them.* 2nd ed. Buffalo, NY: Firefly, 2009. Print. 65.

2. Cailynn Klingbeil. "Arson Analysis Tool Could Speed up Investigations." *Edmonton Journal.* Postmedia Network, 24 Apr. 2014. Web. 25 Apr. 2014.

Source Notes Continued

Chapter 4. Firearms Analysis

1. Douglas Starr. *The Killer of Little Shepherds: A True Crime Story and the Birth of Forensic Science.* New York: Knopf, 2010. Print. 46.

Chapter 5. Written in Blood

1. Colin Evans. *The Father of Forensics: The Groundbreaking Cases of Sir Bernard Spilsbury, and the Beginnings of Modern CSI.* New York: Berkley, 2006. Print. 85.

2. Mohamad Salih Jaff. "Higher Frequency of Secretor Phenotype in O Blood Group—Its Benefits in Prevention and/or Treatment of Some Diseases." *International Journal of Nanomedicine* 5 (2010): 902. Print.

Chapter 6. No More Mistaken Identity

1. "New Fingerprint Breakthrough by Forensic Scientists." *University of Leicester.* University of Leicester, 2 June 2008. Web. 12 May 2014.

Chapter 7. Never without a Trace

1. "Paint Data Query (PDQ)." *Royal Canadian Mounted Police.* Royal Canadian Mounted Police, 22 Nov. 2013. Web. 19 May 2014.

2. Suzanne Bell. *Crime and Circumstance: Investigating the History of Forensic Science.* Westport, CT: Praeger, 2008. Print. 193.

Chapter 8. From Page to Screen

1. Katherine Ramsland. "Ballistics: The Science of Guns." *Crime Library*. Turner Entertainment Networks, n.d. Web. 9 May 2014.

2. Ibid.

3. Ibid.

4. Timothy A. Pearson and Tommie W. Singleton. "Fraud and Forensic Accounting in the Digital Environment." *Issues in Accounting Education* 23.4 (2008): 550. Print.

5. Ibid. 549.

6. Simson L. Garfinkel. "Digital Forensics Research: The Next 10 Years." *Digital Investigation* 7 (2010): 65. Print.

7. Jack Batten. *Mind Over Murder: DNA and Other Forensic Adventures*. Toronto: McClelland & Stewart, 1995. Print. 137.

Chapter 9. The Future of Forensics

1. "Unreliable or Improper Forensic Science." *Innocence Project*. Innocence Project, n.d. Web. 5 May 2014.

2. Max M. Houck. "CSI: Reality." *Scientific American* 295.1 (2006): 84–89. Web.

3. Mark Pollitt. "A History of Digital Forensics." *Advances in Digital Forensics VI*. Eds. Kam-Pui Chow and Sujeet Shenoi. New York: Springer, 2010. Print. 11.

4. Simson L. Garfinkel. "Digital Forensics Research: The Next 10 Years." *Digital Investigation* 7 (2010): 69. Print.

5. Paul Rincon. "Forensic Test Can Predict Hair and Eye Colour from DNA." *BBC News*. BBC, 24 Aug. 2012. Web. 26 May 2014.

6. Paul L. Kirk. *Crime Investigation*. 2nd ed. New York: Wiley, 1974. Print. 2.

$$\frac{a+b}{a} = \frac{a}{b} = 1.618$$

About the Author

L. E. Carmichael never outgrew that stage of childhood when nothing is more fun than amazing your friends (and correcting your teachers!) with your stockpile of weird and wonderful facts. While completing her PhD at the University of Alberta, Carmichael performed DNA fingerprinting for 15 wildlife forensic cases and testified as an expert witness. Since then, she has written children's books about everything from hybrid cars to scoliosis, and her 2013 release *Fox Talk* was a Benjamin Franklin Award Silver Medal winner.

$$\frac{a+b}{a} = \frac{a}{b} = 1.618$$